SCHOLASTIC

P9-CFI-979

Perfect Poems
for Teaching Sight Words

Delightful Poems, Research-Based Lessons, and Instant Activities That Teach the Top High-Frequency Words

BY DEBORAH ELLERMEYER AND JUDITH ROWELL

New York • Toronto • London • Auckland • Sydney
Mexico City • New Delhi • Hong Kong • Buenos Aires

Teaching *Resources*

K H

To my father, Paul Sanko, with love and best wishes.
—D.E.

To my husband, Dick, with love.
—J.R.

Cover art and design by Kathy Massaro
Interior design by Solutions by Design, Inc.
Illustration by James Hale

ISBN: 0-439-57404-8
Copyright © 2005 Deborah Ellermeyer and Judith Rowell
Published by Scholastic Inc.
All rights reserved.
Printed in the U.S.A.

3 4 5 6 7 8 9 10   40   13 12 11 10 09 08 07 06

9/19/06

Contents

Welcome to *Perfect Poems for Teaching Sight Words!*

Sight words and poetry are a winning combination! Sight words—words that are recognized at a glance, without decoding—are key to reading success, and the rhythm and rhyme of poetry is a natural invitation into reading. This book brings the two together into one valuable resource.

The poems within this book feature words from the Dolch list, a widely recognized list of sight words (see page 10). The Dolch list is comprised of the 220 most frequently encountered words in books that children read. The Dolch list of the 95 most commonly encountered nouns (see page 12) expands the scope of the first list.

Not only does each poem provide an authentic context for children's experiences with sight words, the poems and companion activities also present an opportunity to introduce children to specific elements of language such as parts of speech, word families, and more. This gives children an opportunity to learn the words in a meaningful context as well as examine them in isolation. (Though each lesson indicates a particular element of language you may not be labeling yet for children, such as antonyms, children will be exploring the language concept at their own developmental level and using it as an organizing principle. For instance, even if you do use the term antonyms, children will still be developing their understanding of opposites.) In addition, many of the activities use the sight words from the poems as springboards to vocabulary building, introducing new words which are not sight words but fit into the target category.

Use the poems and lessons to:

1 **Introduce** beginning readers to new sight words.

2 **Reinforce** previously learned sight words and provide children with reading practice.

3 **Assess** children's retention of sight words. Ask individual children to read selected poems to you, and make note of any words that require additional practice.

4 **Present** language skills as they arise within the language arts curriculum (such as synonyms, antonyms, and parts of speech).

5 **Enrich** learning in other curriculum areas. For example, you might integrate the poem "Counting Circus" into a math unit, or use it to activate prior knowledge before reading a story about the circus.

What Are Sight Words?
Why Focus on Sight Words?

A sight word is a word that is recognized instantly and without word analysis (Richek, Caldwell, Jennings and Lerner, 2002). Many of these high-frequency words are function words, such as *the*, *of*, and *to*, and have little meaning of their own. Consequently, children must learn to recognize them at a glance to increase reading fluency and comprehension. Sight word instruction is essential for emergent, beginning, and struggling readers. Dolch words are commonly taught at the primary level; however, sight word instruction is also an essential component of most remedial reading programs.

Research has long stressed the importance of children's learning sight words, not only in isolation but also in context. Children should be able to instantly recognize the words on flash cards and within sentences. Using patterned and predictable text such as poetry with beginning readers has long been recognized as best practice. Plus, it's lots of fun!

About This Book

The benefits of this book are many. Here are some:

1 **It's easy to use.** Lessons require little preparation and few outside materials. Each unit includes an original poem rich with Dolch sight words as well as several engaging activities that enhance sight word development and the featured language skill. Sight words within the poems are identified by boldface type.

2 **It's versatile.** You can use the poems to introduce sight words, or to review and reinforce previously learned sight words. You can also use the lessons for whole-class or small-group instruction.

3 **The poems are engaging, enjoyable, and authentic.** Children see an immediate purpose for learning the sight

words, since they are needed for the successful reading of the poems. The progression from whole text to words back to whole text allows children to make important connections between the Dolch words and the larger text (Rasinski and Padak, 2000).

4 **Kids get multiple exposures and repetition of sight words.** Word learning requires children to view words repeatedly in a variety of texts (McCormick, 1994, 1995). Many of these poems repeat words and phrases, so that children get multiple opportunities with the sight words.

5 **Poems feature controlled vocabulary, with emphasis on sight words.** Each poem has been carefully composed to include a high percentage of Dolch sight words and a low percentage of non-Dolch words. The non-Dolch words enhance the poems, since many high-frequency words are function words, such as *the*, *of*, and *to*. These words take on meaning only by acting as connectors for other words (Richek, Caldwell, Jennings, and Lerner, 2002).

6 **Text is patterned and predictable, perfect for emergent or beginning readers.** Research has repeatedly demonstrated that the use of patterned and predictable text is extremely beneficial (Rasinski and Padak, 2001). Using predictable materials not only assists in sight word development but encourages children to use context clues when encountering unknown words, and also creates positive feelings about reading aloud (Bridge, Winograd, and Haley, 1983). The rhythmic nature of poetry and the use of rhyme provide a helpful scaffold for children. Children can use background knowledge, context clues, and their own sense of rhythm and rhyme to help them decode unfamiliar words.

7 **Poems can be used for authentic, performance-based assessment.** Poems can be used as an assessment of children's retention of sight words. As children individually read selected poems, you can make note of sight words with which the child needs additional

practice. You may also elect to have individual children read the poems on audiotape. Having children read on tape provides a record of progress over time that can be easily included in the child's portfolio of work samples. You might also use the poems to assess fluency skills and expression.

8 **Enjoyable activities reinforce sight word development.** The activities provide additional practice of sight words, as well as other essential language skills. Rasinski and Padak (2000) stress the need for children to "explore, make, and play with words." The activities are an opportunity for children to do just that. Many of the activities are designed to engage children working in pairs or small groups. This arrangement promotes socialization and overall language usage among children.

Adapting the Poems and Activities for Different Levels

Depending on the age and level of your students, you'll want to adapt the poems and activities as necessary. Older children may benefit from having a copy of the poem page as well as seeing it displayed on chart paper, while younger children will benefit from choral readings of the poem on the chart paper only.

Older children may be able to work independently on some activities, while younger children will need help writing. If you have reading buddies or older students who visit your class, the reproducible activities are ideal for this type of one-on-one work. Younger children might also simply say an answer aloud or dictate as an adult records. In addition, you might do the activities in small groups during reading center time. This way you can work closely with each child and scaffold as necessary.

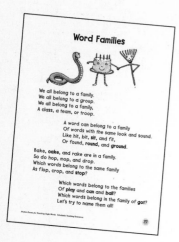

Using the Poems

Follow this simple step-by-step procedure for each poem.

1 **Read the poem in advance.** Preview the poems and activities yourself before you use them with children. This gives you an opportunity to familiarize yourself with the words that will be introduced or reviewed and to select the activity that best suits children's instructional needs.

2 **Write the poem on chart paper and highlight the Dolch words.** Print the poem on chart paper prior to presenting it. Write the target (boldface) words in a different-colored marker to draw children's attention to them. Please note that the boldface words are sight words related to the focus of the lessons, such as *hot* and *cold* for "Antonyms." (There will be non-boldface sight words in the poems as well.)

3 **Point to the words as you read the poem aloud.** Use a pointer or your finger to track the print as you read aloud to the group. This gives children an opportunity to see the words as they are read. You can make pointers easily with a dowel rod and a small decoration added to the tip. For example, an apple eraser makes a good September pointer decoration.

4 **Engage in repeated readings of the poem.** Since children require multiple exposures to new sight words, read the poems repeatedly in a variety of ways: chorally, in two groups with each group reading every other line, and so on. Children might also act out the poems.

5 **Examine selected Dolch words in isolation and in context.** After reading the poem as a whole piece of text several times, children can explore individual words and complete the related activities. Then have children revisit the poem. This progression from whole text, to words, and back to whole text provides children with a necessary and authentic context for learning (Rasinski and Padak, 2000).

6 **Have children write words on index cards and add them to individual Dolch word banks.** Have children create and maintain individual word banks that contain the Dolch words as you introduce them. Word banks are containers (recipe card holders work well), in which children store words in two groups: *Words I Know* and *Words to Learn*. Children file unfamiliar words in the *Words to Learn* section of the container and gradually move words over to the *Words I Know* section. Children can also alphabetize the cards or sort them into groups (words with one or two syllables; nouns, verbs, adjectives, and prepositions; by vowel sound, and so on).

7 **Afterward, keep the poem visible so that children will continue seeing the words.** This ensures multiple exposures to the words. A weekly poetry walk around the classroom is a wonderful way to review the Dolch words within the poems. You might also create a word wall of all the sight words.

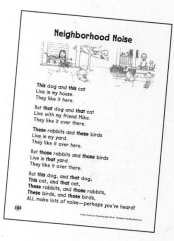

The Dolch 220 Basic Sight Words

a	brown	first	hold
about	but	five	hot
after	buy	fly	how
again	by	for	hurt
all	call	found	I
always	came	four	if
am	can	from	in
an	carry	full	into
and	clean	funny	is
any	cold	gave	it
are	come	get	its
around	could	give	jump
as	cut	go	just
ask	did	goes	keep
at	do	going	kind
ate	does	good	know
away	done	got	laugh
be	don't	green	let
because	down	grow	light
been	draw	had	like
before	drink	has	little
best	eat	have	live
better	eight	he	long
big	every	help	look
black	fall	her	made
blue	far	here	make
both	fast	him	many
bring	find	his	may

Perfect Poems for Teaching Sight Words Scholastic Teaching Resources

me	ran	ten	warm
much	read	thank	was
my	red	that	wash
myself	ride	the	we
never	right	their	well
new	round	them	went
no	run	then	were
not	said	there	what
now	saw	these	when
of	say	they	where
off	see	think	which
old	seven	this	white
on	shall	those	who
once	she	three	why
one	should	to	will
only	show	today	wish
open	sing	together	with
or	sit	too	work
our	six	try	would
out	sleep	two	write
over	small	under	yellow
own	so	up	yes
pick	some	upon	you
play	soon	us	your
please	start	use	
pretty	stop	very	
pull	take	walk	
put	tell	want	

The Dolch 95 Commonly Used Nouns

apple	day	home	school
baby	dog	horse	seed
back	doll	house	sheep
ball	door	kitty	shoe
bear	duck	leg	sister
bed	egg	letter	snow
bell	eye	man	song
bird	farm	men	squirrel
birthday	farmer	milk	stick
boat	father	money	street
box	feet	morning	sun
boy	fire	mother	table
bread	fish	name	thing
brother	floor	nest	time
cake	flower	night	top
car	game	paper	toy
cat	garden	party	tree
chair	girl	picture	watch
chicken	good-bye	pig	water
children	grass	rabbit	way
Christmas	ground	rain	wind
coat	hand	ring	window
corn	head	robin	wood
cow	hill	Santa Claus	

Perfect Poems for Teaching Sight Words Scholastic Teaching Resources

The
Poems
&
Activities

We Are Opposites

We are opposites,
And I'll tell you more!
I say **after**,
And you say **before**.

I look **up**,
And you look **down**.
I like to **walk**,
You **run** to town.

I say **stop**,
And you say **go**.
We are opposites—
I told you so!

I think it's **hot**,
You think it's **cold**.
I say it's **new**,
You say it's **old**.

I come **in**,
And you go **out**.
We are opposites,
Let's give a shout!

I am **small**,
As **small** as can be.
You are **big**,
Much bigger than me.

We are opposites,
It's like I said before.
Think of your own,
If you want any more!

14

Using the Poem

Activity 1

Ollie's Opposites

Sight Word Focus

Antonyms

Objectives

- to understand the concept of opposites
- to use or guess sight words that are opposites correctly in a pantomime

Setup

- Draw a simple outline of an octopus onto posterboard and cut out. Tape to the chalkboard or wall and write "Ollie" on the head. Copy page 16 for each child.
- Write the following words on separate index cards so that you have 16 cards total: *after/before, up/down, hot/cold, walk/run, new/old, stop/go, small/big,* and *out/in.*

MATERIALS

- copies of octopus pattern (page 16), one per child
- posterboard
- 8 large paper clips or clothespins
- 16 3- by 5-inch index cards
- scissors
- marker

Directions

1 Read each index card aloud with the class. Distribute the cards (one per child, 16 children can play at once).

2 Distribute copies of page 16. Tell children they will record word pairs during the game they are about to play.

3 Invite one child to pantomime his or her word, using gestures only. The group guesses the word. The child holding that word's opposite comes up and joins the first child. They both show their cards to the group.

4 The pair clips their cards onto one octopus arm. On their sheets, children record the words on one octopus leg. Continue until Ollie has "collected" eight pairs of opposites.

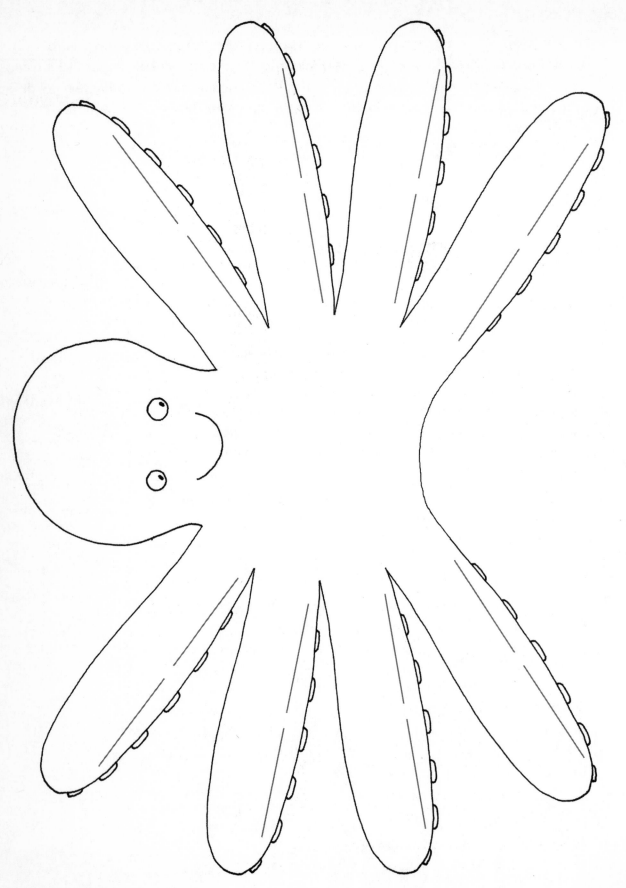

Ollie's Opposites

Perfect Poems for Teaching Sight Words Scholastic Teaching Resources

Opposites Pyramid

Objective

❁ to identify the antonym of a given sight word

Setup

❁ Copy one Opposites Pyramid page per child.

❁ Write the first word of each of the following pairs on the chalkboard: **black/white, him/her, he/she, to/from, after/before, give/take, yes/no, up/down, out/in, new/old, under/over, hot/cold, little/big, on/off, start/stop, bring/take, come/go, came/went, do/don't, run/walk, always/never, long**/short, **light**/heavy, **full**/empty, **far**/near, **clean**/dirty, **right**/wrong, **sit**/stand, **pull**/push, **many**/few, **gave**/took, lost/**found**, **first**/last, **fast**/slow, **all**/none, **good**/bad, **open**/close, high/low, lose/win, better/worse.

(boldface indicates Dolch list words)

❁ Using a marker, write the *second word* of each pair above on a 3- by 5-inch index card and place a hat, bag or box.

MATERIALS

○ copies of page 18 (one per child)

○ 10 counters (bingo chips or dry beans) per child

○ 40 3- by 5-inch index cards

○ hat, bag or box

○ marker

○ chalk

Directions

1 Distribute an Opposites Pyramid page and 10 counters to each child.

2 Have children randomly select words from the list on the chalkboard and write each in a space on the pyramid. Each child's pyramid will look different, as on a Bingo card.

3 Place the word cards in a hat, bag or box. Randomly draw one card at a time. Say the word, show it to children, and direct them to think of the opposite of that word. If the child has that word on the pyramid, he or she covers the space with a counter.

4 Continue drawing cards until a child has filled the pyramid, at which time he or she raises a hand and says, "Pyramid!"

5 In order to check the answers, the child should say each covered word and its opposite.

6 Have children exchange papers and play again.

Opposites Pyramid

Perfect Poems for Teaching Sight Words Scholastic Teaching Resources

Color With Me

Yellow, blue, black, and **green,**
  Brown, red, and **white.**
Which of these seven colors
  Would be just right?
To color the sun
  Way up in the sky?
To color the water
  That passes us by?

To color the night
  As dark as can be?
To color the grass
  That grows under me?

To color the dirt
  In the flower bed?
To color the apple
  That falls on my head?

To color the snow
  That we use to make
a snow angel, a snowball,
  And a great big snow cake?

Yellow, blue, black, and **green,**
  Brown, red, and **white.**
Which of these seven colors
  Would be just right?

Using the Poem

Begin by writing the poem "Color With Me" on chart paper. Write the color words in a corresponding colored marker. Ask several children to name a favorite color. While reading the poem, pause and ask children to identify the colors suggested in each stanza of the poem. In addition, have them identify classroom objects that are the color mentioned. See pages 8–9 for ideas on sharing the poem.

(NOTE: Before beginning any work with colors, determine whether any children in the class are color blind.)

Sight Word Focus

Color Words

MATERIALS

○ copies of page 21 (one per child)

○ crayons or markers

Activity 1

Draw Me a Color

Objectives

❋ to select and use the correct color to draw a picture

❋ to recognize sight words for colors

Setup

Copy and distribute the Draw Me a Color reproducible to children.

Directions

1 Ask children to read and follow the directions. Have them use crayons or markers to complete the page. Together, you might brainstorm things in each color group.

2 Then invite each child to draw his or her own picture in the last box and write its color on the line. Have children share their drawings when complete.

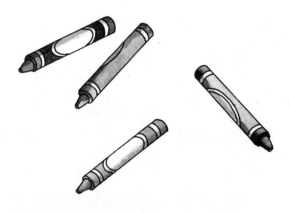

20

Perfect Poems for Teaching Sight Words Scholastic Teaching Resources

Name: _____   Date: _____

Draw Me a Color

Read and follow the directions for each box.

Draw a small **yellow** ball.	Draw a **brown** cow.
Draw a **blue** cat.	Draw a **red** apple.
Draw a **black** fly.	Draw a **white** snowman.
Draw a **green** bug.	Draw your own picture. Write its color on the line. _____

Guess the Color

Sight Word Focus

Color Words

MATERIALS

○ chart paper or chalkboard

○ copies of page 23 (one per child)

○ paper and pencils

Objectives

❀ to write sight words for colors

❀ to create a color riddle

Setup

Copy and distribute page 23. Write the color sight words on chart paper or on the chalkboard. To provide support for younger children, you might print the color words in the corresponding colors.

Directions

1 Direct children's attention to the color words written on the chart paper or chalkboard. Review the words. Tell children that they will be using these words to answer color riddles.

2 Read each color riddle together several times. Then have children write the answers to the riddles on their papers.

3 When you have finished reading all the riddles, go over the answers to the riddles and have children tell why they chose each answer. Ask, *Are there other colors that could answer each riddle? Tell why or why not.*

4 Have children write their own color riddles and share them with the class. Remind them that their riddles do not need to rhyme.

Name: _____ Date: _____

Color Riddles

Read the riddles. Write the answers on the lines.

A dandelion,
cold lemonade,
a drawing of the sun
that I just made.
What color am I?

_____

Billy's eyes,
the color of sky,
round little berries
in a fresh-baked pie.
What color am I?

_____

Your eyes are open,
but you can barely see.
The night is dark,
just right for me.
What color am I?

_____

I am veggies and fruit,
dollars and peas.
I'm the soft grass
beneath your feet.
What color am I?

_____

An apple, a valentine,
a big strawberry,
a nose when it's cold,
a nice sweet cherry.
What color am I?

_____

Write your own riddle:

_____

_____

_____

_____

_____

_____

_____

Monkeys, seedpods,
bark on trees,
squishy mud,
old dried leaves.
What color am I?

_____

My pearly teeth,
the polar bear,
it's kind of a color
that isn't there.
What color am I?

_____

Jungle Colors

Sight Word Focus

Color Words

Objective

⬡ to match the correct sight word with its color

Setup

⬡ Copy and distribute page 25 (one per child).

⬡ Cut sheets of yellow, blue, green, red, white, and brown construction paper into 1-inch squares.

⬡ Place a square of each color in the bags and distribute (one per child).

MATERIALS

○ copies of page 25 (one per child)

○ 1-inch colored construction paper squares: yellow, blue, green, red, white, brown (one of each per child)

○ scissors

○ small, self-sealing plastic bags (one per child)

○ crayons or markers

○ glue sticks

Directions

1 Have children take out their crayons. Make sure that each child has one of each of the following color crayons: yellow, blue, green, red, white (optional), and brown.

2 Tell children to look at the Jungle Colors page and notice the color words written in the boxes. Say each color as children point to the words.

3 Direct children to match each color square in the plastic bag to the correct color word on the jungle scene by placing it on the page and gluing it down.

4 Have children color the objects the correct color. Children can either leave the white flowers blank or color them with a white crayon.

5 Once children are done with the six colors, they may continue coloring the rest of the picture.

Jungle Colors

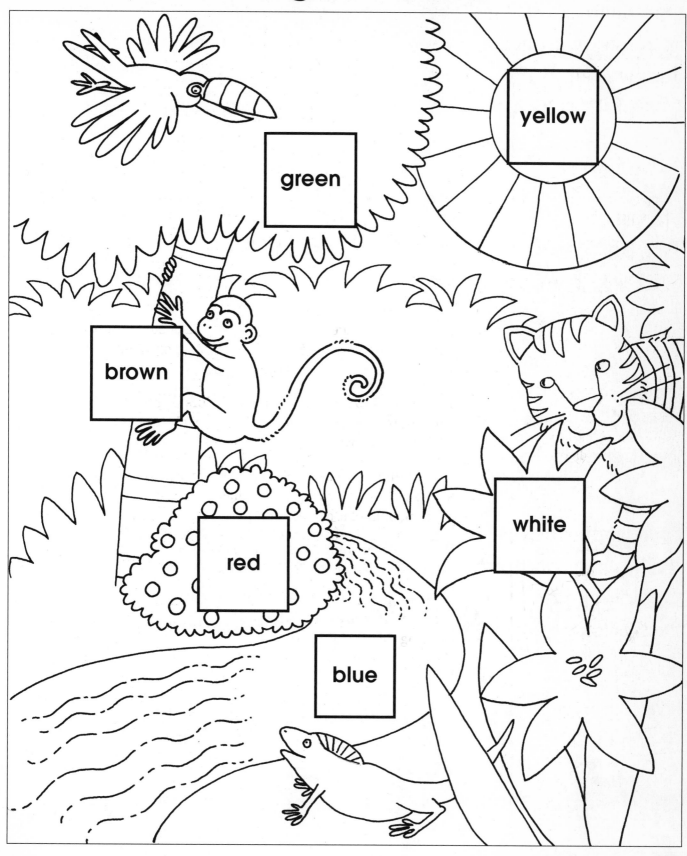

Counting Circus

One funny clown
With **one** funny nose,
Juggles **one** ball
In his big, big clothes.

Two balloons fly
Up, up, and away.
Two balloons fly,
But I wish they could stay!

Three circus rings,
Count them with me.
Three round rings,
What else do I see?

Four white dogs
Walk, jump, and play.
One black cat
Runs quickly away.

Five children laugh
At the circus show.
Asking, "Oh, no!
Is it time to go?"

Six red balls
Tossed up in the sky.
Two hands catch them
As they fly by.

Seven bears dance
Way up on their toes.
One falls down,
Right on his bear nose!

Eight red apples
On short brown sticks
Are eaten by children
As **eight** clowns do tricks.

Nine bags of popcorn,
They feel so warm.
Outside, **nine** clouds gather
For a summer rainstorm.

It's now **ten** o'clock,
And it's time to go.
Thank you for coming
To the circus show!

Perfect Poems for Teaching Sight Words Scholastic Teaching Resources

Using the Poem

Write the poem "Counting Circus" on chart paper, writing the number words in a different-colored marker. As you read the poem aloud (see pages 8–9 for tips on sharing the poem), ask children to raise the correct number of fingers each time they hear a number word. You might also pause at each number word and ask children questions such as: *What number comes before this one? What number comes after it? Is this number even or odd?*

Activity 1

Ben's Number Soup

Sight Word Focus

Number Words

MATERIALS

- copies of page 28 (one per child)
- copies of page 29 (one per child)
- chart paper
- markers
- scissors
- glue sticks

Objectives

- to associate numerical amounts with number words
- to read the sight words for numerals
- to create original number stories

Setup

- Write the "Ben's Number Soup" story (below right) on chart paper.
- Duplicate and distribute to each child the soup bowl and vegetable reproducibles (pages 28–29). Also provide children with scissors and glue sticks.

Directions

1 Read "Ben's Number Soup" (see box, right) aloud with children. After reading, review the numerals and number words used in the story.

2 Next, tell children they can help Ben make the soup. Direct their attention to the number soup recipe and read it aloud together. Ask children to point to each vegetable picture to make sure they can identify it.

3 Have children cut out and fit their vegetables in the bowl, then glue them into place. Circulate to check children's work as they go.

4 On the back of the page, children can create their own soup "recipes" by gluing on different amounts of leftover vegetable cutouts. Tell children to write the appropriate number words (one through ten) beside each ingredient.

BEN'S NUMBER SOUP

Ben loves soup. He eats it every day. One day, Ben's mother asked him to help her make vegetable soup. She asked him to read the list of ingredients and tell her how many she needed of each vegetable. Ben knew the numerals 1, 2, 3, 4, 5, 6, 7, 8, 9, and 10, but the numbers were written as words instead: *one, two, three, four, five, six, seven, eight, nine,* and *ten.*

Ben's Number Soup

Cut out and glue the correct number of each vegetable in Ben's soup bowl.

- **four** carrots
- **three** string beans
- **one** cabbage
- **five** peas
- **seven** celery sticks
- **ten** tomatoes
- **two** cobs of corn
- **nine** onions
- **six** potatoes
- **eight** lima beans

Perfect Poems for Teaching Sight Words Scholastic Teaching Resources

Vegetables

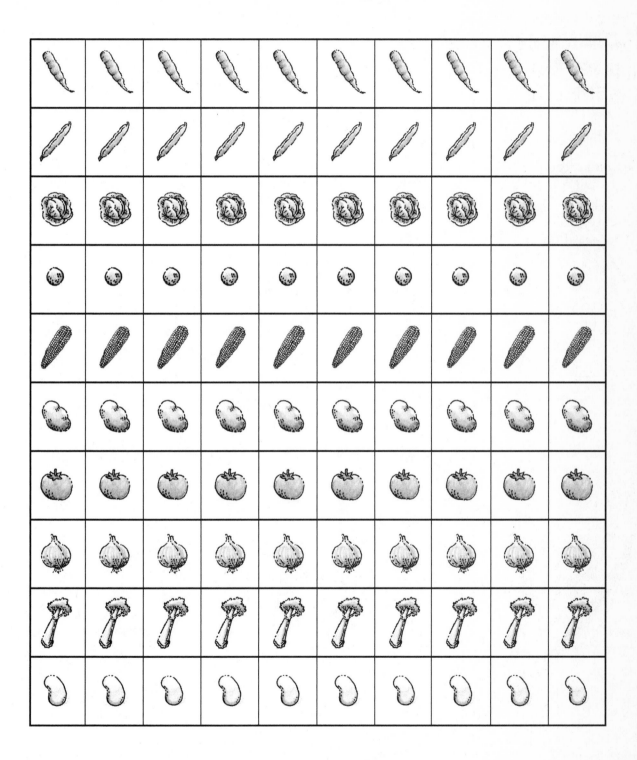

Activity 2

What's Hiding?

Objectives

⬢ to distinguish number words from non-number words

⬢ to write number words from one through ten

Setup

Copy and distribute page 31 (one per child). Alternatively, create a transparency and place the page on an overhead, or write the text on chart paper.

Directions

1 Direct children's attention to the activity page, transparency, or chart. Have children read each set of words carefully and cross out the word in each set that does not belong. (If children will be completing the activity individually, you might work through the first set as a group.)

2 Next, have children write a number word on the line at the end of each list. Children may write any number word from one through ten that is not already on the list.

3 When children are finished, help them check their work.

MATERIALS

○ copies of page 31 (one per child)

○ pencils or transparency marker

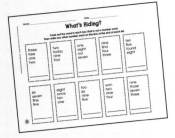

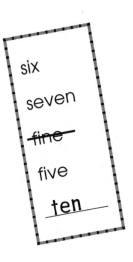

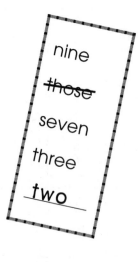

Name: _____

What's Hiding?

**Cross out the word in each box that is *not* a number word.
Then write any other number word on the line at the end of each list.**

ten five found eight _____	nine those seven three _____
nine find four three _____	won two nine four _____
one eight our seven _____	too six nine five _____
two today nine four _____	eight once ten one _____
three tree one two _____	six seven fine five _____

The Little, Little Man

In a **big, big** city,
Lived a **little, little** man,
In his **hot, hot** house,
With a **fast, fast** fan.

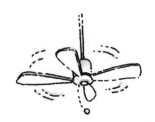

He had **funny, funny** children,
And a **pretty, pretty** wife.
They would laugh, laugh, laugh,
What a **good, good** life!

They would run around the house,
They would say jokes and rhymes.
They would jump up and down,
And have happy, happy times.

Do you know this **little** man?
Oh, whoever could he be?
Why, that **little, little** man
Is just silly, silly me!

Perfect Poems for Teaching Sight Words Scholastic Teaching Resources

Using the Poem

Write the poem "The Little, Little Man" on chart paper, using a different colored marker for the highlighted words. Read the poem aloud with children (see pages 8–9 for step-by-step instructions). Then invite children to perform an echo reading of the poem by reading one line at a time and having them repeat it after you. As you read, point out each highlighted word.

Activity 1

Super Synonyms

Sight Word Focus

Synonyms

Objectives

🌸 to understand that synonyms are words with similar meanings

🌸 to brainstorm synonyms for target sight words

🌸 to recognize that synonyms can have different degrees of meaning

MATERIALS

○ chart paper

○ markers

○ sticky notes

Setup

Display the chart paper poem you created for "The Little, Little Man" (see Using the Poem, above).

Directions

1 Discuss the concept of synonyms. Explain to children that synonyms are words that mean about the same thing.

2 Call children's attention to the word *big* in the first line and write the word on the chart paper. Then invite children to suggest other words that mean about the same thing (*large, huge, enormous, giant, jumbo,* and so on). Write children's ideas on the chart paper underneath the word *big*.

3 Review the list of synonyms together and ask children if they think there are any differences among the words. For example, ask: *Which is bigger, something that is* large *or something that is* enormous? Repeat steps 2 and 3 for each highlighted word in the poem.

4 Rewrite the poem together, using sticky notes to replace the highlighted words with different synonyms from the lists. Read the new poem aloud together.

Odd Word Out

Objectives

🌸 to identify synonyms for target sight words

🌸 to choose the word that does not belong to a set of synonyms

🌸 to state a synonym that belongs to a set of synonyms

Setup

Print each word below on an index card. You might use a different color for each set of words.

Set 1: big, large, **tiny**   Set 9: pretty, cute, **ugly**

Set 2: little, **large**, small   Set 10: cold, **hot**, icy

Set 3: start, begin, **stop**   Set 11: fast, quick, **slow**

Set 4: away, gone, **here**   Set 12: many, lots, **few**

Set 5: go, **come**, leave   Set 13: sleep, nap, **wake**

Set 6: jump, **swim**, hop   Set 14: going, **coming**, leaving

Set 7: run, dash, **walk**   Set 15: pull, **push**, tug

Set 8: hot, **cold**, warm   Set 16: may, **don't**, can

Directions

1 Discuss synonyms. Guide children to understand that synonyms are words that have the same general meaning. Divide the class into pairs.

2 Give each pair a set of three prepared index cards.

3 Tell children to read the three words and decide which word doesn't belong in the set.

4 Invite each pair to stand in front of the group, show their cards, and say which one does not belong. Ask the group to suggest words that could belong to the remaining pair.

Sight Word Focus

Synonyms

MATERIALS

○ 48 index cards

○ markers

Synonym Pairs

Objective

❀ to rewrite the poem "The Little, Little Man" with synonyms

Setup

Copy page 36 for each pair of children.

Directions

1 Divide the group into pairs. Distribute copies of page 36 to each pair.

2 Ask children to work together to fill in the blanks with "synonym pairs"—for instance, "the *Silly, Funny* Man" or "In a *loud, noisy* city."

3 After children have rewritten the poems, they can illustrate them on separate sheets of paper.

4 Have children read their poems aloud to their group.

Sight Word Focus

Synonyms

MATERIALS

○ copies of page 36 (one per pair)

○ pencils

○ crayons

○ paper

The _____, _____ Man

In a _____ , _____ city

Lived a _____ , _____ man,

In his _____ , _____ house,

With one _____ , _____ fan.

He had _____ , _____ children,

And a _____ , _____ wife.

They would laugh, laugh, laugh.

What a _____ , _____ life!

They would run around the house.

They would say jokes and rhymes.

They would jump up and down,

And have _____ , _____ times.

Do you know this little man?

Oh, whoever could he be?

Why, that _____ , _____ man

Is just _____ , _____ me!

Perfect Poems for Teaching Sight Words Scholastic Teaching Resources

I'm All Mixed Up

I'm all mixed up.
I need help from you.
How do I **no / know**
Why the sky is **blue / blew**?
I do not **no / know**.
I wish I **new / knew**!

Is my sister aged **for / four** or **too / to / two**?
Eye / I am named Marie.
She is named **Be / Bee / Bea**.
We eat **red / read** berries
By the water at the **see / sea**.

I have a lot of work to **do / due**!
I'll **so / sew** a button
on the coat you **wear / where**.
I'll sit on that chair.
I'll wait **right / write** over **there / their**.

I'm all mixed up.
I need help from you.
Can you choose the right words?
See what you can do!

Write the poem "I'm All Mixed Up" on chart paper, using a different-colored marker for the highlighted homophones. Tell the class that you will need their help in correcting the poem. Share the poem with children and then have them read it chorally. (See pages 8–9 for tips on sharing the poems.) NOTE: Sets of boldface words contain both Dolch and Non-Dolch words.

Sight Word Focus

Homophones

MATERIALS

○ none

Activity 1

Homophone Help

Objectives

❋ to recognize sight words that are homophones

❋ to use homophones correctly in a sentence

Setup

Display the chart paper poem you created for "I'm All Mixed Up" (see Using the Poem, above).

Directions

1 After reading the poem once through, ask, *Why is the person in the poem confused?*

2 Engage children in a discussion of the meaning of each homophone. Point out how the homophones in each group are alike (they sound the same when read aloud) and different (they are spelled differently and have different meanings).

3 Help children identify which homophones belong in the poem. Circle the correct word in each line.

4 Next, encourage volunteers to use each circled homophone in a sentence of their own, then use the uncircled homophone in a sentence.

Our Homophone Book

Objective

❀ to write and illustrate sentences for homophones

Directions

1 Choose a homophone pair from the poem or from the box below and write a sentence on the chalkboard using each homophone.

2 Tell children that they will be writing and illustrating their own homophone sentences and creating a class book. Divide the class into pairs and assign each pair a homophone pair. Have them fold their papers in half and write a sentence for each homophone on either side. Children can then illustrate their sentences.

3 When children are finished, bind all the pages together into a class book. Read the book together.

Sight Word Focus

Homophones

MATERIALS

○ paper
○ stapler or "O" ring
○ crayons
○ markers
○ pencils

More Homophone Pairs

❀ pairs/pear
❀ knot/not
❀ aunt/ant
❀ ate/ant
❀ flour/flower
❀ weight/wait

❀ brake/break
❀ cent/sent
❀ days/daze
❀ facts/fax
❀ toes/tows
❀ buy/by

Homophone Stories

Sight Word Focus

Homophones

Objective

🌀 to locate homophones in picture books

Setup

Gather a collection of picture books that contain homophones in the text (see below left). Divide the class into small groups and distribute one book to each group, along with writing paper and pencils.

Directions

1 Have children write the titles of their books at the top of their papers.

2 Then encourage children to take turns reading the book aloud to each other. As they read, have them search for homophones in the text.

3 Invite children to list any pairs of homophones they find. (Be sure children understand that the homophones do not have to appear next to each other in the book.)

4 Children might also list words that they know homophones for, even if the corresponding homophone does not appear in the book. For example, if children spot only the word *to*, they might add the words *too/two* to their lists.

5 When partners are finished, have them share their homophones with the class.

MATERIALS

○ picture books (one per small group)

○ writing paper

○ pencils

Picture Books Featuring Homonyms

The Moose Is in the Mousse by Pam Scheunemann (SandCastle, 2002)

Sam Has a Sundae on Sunday by Pam Scheunemann (SandCastle, 2002)

Harry Is Not Hairy by Pam Scheunemann (SandCastle, 2002)

The King Who Rained by Fred Gwynne (Aladdin, 1988)

A Chocolate Moose for Dinner by Fred Gwynne (Aladdin, 1988)

Eight Ate: A Feast of Homonym Riddles by Marvin Terban (Clarion Books, 1982)

All About You

Who are you?
Do you have a name?
Who are you?
How are we the same?

What do you do
After school is done?
What do you do
In the rain, snow, and sun?

Where do you go
With your very best friends?
Where do you go
When the school week ends?

How do you get to school?
In a car or bus?
How do you get to school?
You can walk with us!

Which kind of books
Do you read each day?
Books about people,
Or lands far away?

When do you go
To sleep every night?
When do you wake up?
Is the time just right?

Why do I ask these questions?
Why do I want to find out?
Because we are alike, yet different.
And that's what it's all about!

Using the Poem

Write the poem "All About You" on chart paper, highlighting the question words with a different-colored marker. Read the poem aloud once through and ask children what they notice about the highlighted words. After eliciting that these are question words, reread the poem and invite children to chime in on those words. (For tips on sharing the poems, see pages 8–9.)

Sight Word Focus

Question Words

MATERIALS

○ copies of page 43 (one per child)

○ pencils

Activity 1

Who Are You?

Objectives

❈ to use sight words that are question words in classmate interviews

❈ to introduce a classmate to the group using information gathered from the interview

Setup

Duplicate and distribute the Interview Form (page 43), one to each child. Then divide the class into pairs. You might partner children with classmates they do not often spend time with.

Directions

1 Review the highlighted question words from the poem with children. Explain that we can use these words when we meet new people to find out about them.

2 Invite pairs of children to take turns interviewing each other, using the questions on the Interview Form. Have children write their partner's responses on the lines.

3 After partners have completed their interviews, they can take turns "introducing" each other to the class. Encourage children to use the information from the interview in their introductions.

My Name: _____ Partner's Name: _____

Date: _____

Interview Form

1. **Who** are you? Tell your first, middle, and last name.

   _____

2. **What** is your favorite thing to do after school?

   _____

   _____

3. **Where** is your favorite place to go on the weekend?

   _____

   _____

4. **How** do you get to school most days?

   _____

   _____

5. **Which** is your favorite kind of book to read—books about people, animals, or places?

   _____

   _____

6. **When** do you go to sleep on school nights?
   When do you get up in the morning?

   _____

   _____

Perfect Poems for Teaching Sight Words Scholastic Teaching Resources

Newspaper Scavenger Hunt

Sight Word Focus

Question Words

MATERIALS

- multiple copies of five or six different newspaper or magazine articles (one copy per child within each group)
- highlighter pens (one per child)

Objectives

- to locate information in a newspaper article
- to summarize the article by answering key questions

Setup

Locate five to six different newspaper articles with photos (from a school newspaper or classroom magazine). Copy each article for use in small groups. Then write the following six questions on the chalkboard:

What happened in the story?

When did it happen?

Where did it happen?

Why did it happen?

How did it happen?

Who was involved?

Directions

1 Divide the class into five to six groups, one group for each set of newspaper articles.

2 Provide each group with a different article, one copy per child. Also provide each child with a highlighter pen.

3 Direct children's attention to the key questions on the chalkboard and read them aloud as a class.

4 Encourage children to read the article together and find the answers to the questions. Have each child highlight the key information on his or her copy of the article.

5 When children are finished, have each group work together to prepare a presentation of the information they found. You might like to have each child in the group choose one of the six questions to answer for the class.

My Busy Day

I **run**. I **ride**.
I **read** and **write**.
I **pick**. I **pull**.
I **fly** a kite.

I **open** and close.
I touch my nose.
I **carry** a sled
In case it snows.

I **give** a gift.
I **tell** a tale.
I **see** a sign.
I shout, "For sale!"

I **clean**. I **wash**.
I **eat** so I'll **grow**.
Who **makes** my food?
I **want** to know.

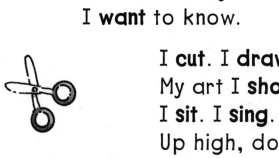

I **cut**. I **draw**.
My art I **show**.
I **sit**. I **sing**.
Up high, down low.

I **look**. I **jump**.
I **find** a nest.
I trip. I **fall**.
I need a rest!

From day to night
I **keep** on the go.
I close my eyes
To **sleep**! Shh! Tiptoe!

Using the Poem

Write the poem "My Busy Day" on chart paper, using a different-colored marker for the highlighted verbs. As you read the poem for the first time, ask children to close their eyes and imagine each action. Then have them open their eyes. Read the poem once more, inviting children to chime in on each action word. Explain to children that action words are called verbs. (For tips on sharing the poem, see pages 8–9.)

Sight Word Focus
Verbs

MATERIALS

○ index cards
○ hat, bag, or box
○ paper
○ chart paper
○ marker
○ pencils

Activity 1

Mime Action

Objectives

❋ to read and write sight words that are action words
❋ to act out verbs and identify verbs acted out by others

Setup

Write each verb from the poem on chart paper, then write each on an index card. Place the index cards in a hat, bag, or box.

Directions

1 Have a child choose a card from the hat, bag, or box without peeking. Encourage him or her to silently read the secret verb and then pantomime the action for the whole group.

2 When children think they know what verb is being pantomimed, have them write it on a sheet of paper. They can refer to the list on chart paper.

3 Once all children have written their guesses, have the "mime" call on a classmate to tell his or her guess. If the guess is correct, that child gets up and chooses the next verb from the hat, bag, or box.

4 Continue play according to children's interest. Children can even brainstorm a new list of verbs and play again!

Activity 2

Today and Yesterday

Objective

❋ to distinguish between sight words that are present and past tense verbs

Setup

Display the chart paper poem you created for "My Busy Day" (see Using the Poem, page 46). Post a blank sheet of chart paper next to the poem.

Directions

1 Reread the poem together and remind children that each highlighted word names an action. Ask: *When does the action in the poem take place? Is it happening today, or did it happen yesterday?* Explain that each action word is in the present tense—that means it is happening now, or today.

2 Reread the poem, this time inserting the word *Today* before each line that contains an action word.

3 Next, ask children: *What would happen to the action words if we began each line with* Yesterday? *How would they change?* Explain that to describe actions that happened yesterday, each action word (verb) needs be past tense: *run* changes to *ran, fly* changes to *flew,* and so on.

4 Work together to write each past tense verb on a separate sheet of chart paper. Then read a new version of the poem, starting each line with *Yesterday* and inserting the past tense verbs. You might point out that some past tense verbs are spelled the same but pronounced differently (*read*) and some are exactly the same (*cut*).

Sight Word Focus

Verbs

MATERIALS

○ chart paper

○ markers

On the Double

MATERIALS

○ chart paper
○ marker
○ writing paper
○ pencils

Objectives

❂ to recognize sight words that are double-usage words (words that are both verbs and nouns)

❂ to use double-usage words correctly in sentences

Setup

Display the chart paper poem you created for "My Busy Day" (see Using the Poem, page 46). Post a blank sheet of chart paper next to the poem and distribute writing paper and pencils to children.

Directions

1 Remind children that a verb names an action. Then explain that a noun names a person, place, thing, or idea. Read the poem aloud, asking children if they see any words that can be both verbs and nouns.

2 Work together to list each double-usage word from the poem on chart paper (*ride, pick, fly, cut, show, look, jump, fall, sleep*).

3 Next, show how to use the words both ways: as verbs and nouns. Write example sentences on chart paper—for instance: *The ride on the roller coaster was exciting. I ride to school on the school bus.* Ask children to tell which *ride* names an action (verb) and which *ride* names a thing (noun).

4 Then have children choose three words from the list and write two sentences for each—one using the word as a verb and one using the word as a noun.

5 When children are finished, have them share their sentences with the class. Encourage the group to tell whether the word is being used as a noun or a verb in each sentence.

Me, You, and Them

He is a boy, and
His name is Jim.
If this toy is **his**, then
It belongs to **him**.

She is a girl, and
Her name is Sue.
Hers is the boat
That is painted blue.

You are **you**.
That is plain to see.
I am not **you**,
And **you** are not **me**!

We are together.
We are more than one.
Please come join **us**
In **our** fun!

"**They**" describes others.
They are more than one.
They walk and talk together.
Together **they** play and run.

I am **me**,
And **I** am special as can be.
You are **my** friend.
Together, **you** and **I** are **we**!

Using the Poem

Write the poem "Me, You, and Them" on chart paper, highlighting the personal pronouns with a different-colored marker. Read the poem to children as you point to the words (for step-by-step instructions on sharing poems, see pages 8–9). Then reread the poem, dividing the class into two groups and alternating stanzas. Finally, call children's attention to the highlighted words. Explain that pronouns are words that stand in for names of people and objects.

Sight Word Focus

Personal Pronouns

MATERIALS

○ index cards

○ hat, bag, or box

Activity 1

Pick a Pronoun

Objectives

❋ to recognize sight words that are personal pronouns as words that stand in for names of people and objects

❋ to distinguish between singular and plural pronouns

❋ to use pronouns in spoken language

Setup

Display the chart paper poem you created for "Me, You, and Them" (see Using the Poem, above). Then write each of the following pronouns on an index card: *me, you, them, he, his, it, him, she, her, hers, I, they, we, us, our,* and *my*. Place the cards in a hat, bag, or box.

Directions

1 After reading the poem together, ask children which highlighted words refer to people (*I, we, they, he, she,* and so on) and which word refers to things (*it*).

2 Make a list of pronouns on the board. Discuss which pronouns refer to one person or thing (singular) and which refer to more than one (plural).

3 Next, invite children to take turns choosing a pronoun card from the hat, bag, or box. Have each child use the word he or she picked in a sentence.

Lift-the-Flap Pronouns

Objective

❖ to write a sight word pronoun and use it correctly in a sentence

Setup

Write the following pronouns on the chalkboard: *I, me, it, my, we, you, he, our, she, they, her, him, his, them, it, us, your,* and *their.*

Directions

1 Provide each child with a sheet of construction paper and have children fold it lengthwise down the middle.

2 Next, help children cut slits in the top half of the sheet, dividing it into six equal sections. This will create a simple lift-the-flap book with six flaps.

3 Encourage each child to choose any six pronouns from the list on the board and write one on each of the six flaps.

4 Then have children lift each flap and write a sentence using the pronoun in the space underneath. Have children underline the pronoun in the sentence.

5 Invite children to share their work by exchanging books and reading the sentences aloud.

Sight Word Focus

Personal Pronouns

MATERIALS

○ 8 1/2- by 11-inch sheets of light construction paper

○ scissors

○ pencils

Pronoun Search

Sight Word Focus

Personal Pronouns

MATERIALS

- index cards
- markers
- pushpins or tape
- variety of texts, such as textbooks, picture books, newspapers, and magazines

Objectives

❋ to identify sight word pronouns in text

❋ to create a classroom word wall of pronouns

Setup

Gather a variety of texts that children use—anything from picture books to the school newsletter. Set out index cards and markers, and make space available on a bulletin board or classroom wall.

Directions

1 Show children the texts and invite them to go on a pronoun hunt. If they like, children can also search for pronouns in environmental print, such as classroom signs and posters.

2 As children find pronouns, have them write the words on index cards. Challenge each child to find as many as he or she can without repeating any words.

3 Display the word cards on a classroom wall or bulletin board.

4 Use the word wall to reinforce children's sight word recognition. Simply point to random cards with a laser pointer or flashlight, and have children read the words aloud.

My Game

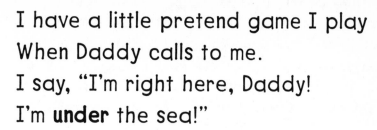

I have a little pretend game I play
When Daddy calls to me.
I say, "I'm right here, Daddy!
I'm **under** the sea!"

Or I say, "I'm **in** the window."
Or else, "I'm **out** the door."
"I'm **on top of** the table,"
Or "I'm **under** the floor."

I say, "I'm right here, Daddy!
I'm **next to** the fish!"
The fish who's swimming
Around his little dish.

I'm jumping **over** boxes,
Or **off** a big red cube.
I'm climbing **up** a tree,
Or swimming **with** my inner tube!

I say, "I'm right here, Daddy!
I'm hiding **by** the door."
And our dog has just come **in**
From a terrible rainstorm!

Now I'm tired of this game.
Let's read "Once **upon** a time."
"Now I'm right here, Daddy.
Into your lap I'll climb."

Using the Poem

Write the poem "My Game" on chart paper, using a different-colored marker for the highlighted prepositions or prepositional phrases. Share the poem with children (for detailed tips on sharing poems, see pages 8–9). Then ask children what they notice about the highlighted words. Explain that these words tell about the position of things, or where things are. They are called prepositions or prepositional phrases. (NOTE: In the poem, the Non-Dolch word *next* is shown in boldface because it is part of a prepositional phrase with *to*.)

Sight Word Focus

Prepositions

MATERIALS

○ copies of page 55 (one per child)

Activity 1

Where Is Everyone?

Objective

❋ to recognize and create prepositional phrases using sight words in a song

Setup

Duplicate the song sheet for "Where Is Everyone?" (page 55) and distribute to children.

Directions

1 First, familiarize children with the tune by singing "Frère Jacques" (or "Are You Sleeping?"). Then tell children they will be learning new words to the song. Read the words on the song sheet together several times, until children are familiar with the pattern.

2 Then sing the song "Where Is Everyone?" together, inserting a child's name in the blank. Have that child hide under his or her desk!

3 Point out the highlighted phrase "under the desk." Explain that this is a *prepositional phrase*—it tells the location, or position, of the person in the song.

4 Then sing the song several more times, inserting different children's names and substituting "under the desk" with the other prepositional phrases on the sheet. Children go to the place described.

5 As children become more familiar with prepositional phrases, invite them to invent their own and lead the class in a new verse.

Where Is Everyone?

(Sing to the tune of "Frère Jacques," or "Are You Sleeping?")

Where is _____?

Where is _____?

Under the desk.

Under the desk.

When I look I'll find him/her.

When I look I'll find him/her.

Under the desk.

Under the desk.

Sing the song again. Replace **under the desk**
with one of these phrases:

with his/her friend

by the window

on the floor

out the door

upon the rug

at the math center

next to me

in the reading nook

Design a Room

Sight Word Focus

Prepositions

MATERIALS

- large sheets of construction paper
- old magazines
- scissors
- glue sticks
- crayons
- pencils

Objectives

❀ to orally describe a room, using sight word prepositions

❀ to write a descriptive paragraph, using prepositions

Setup

❀ Display the chart paper poem you created for "My Game" (see Using the Poem, page 54).

❀ Write the prepositions and prepositional phrases from the poem on the chalkboard.

❀ Provide children with construction paper, old magazines, scissors, glue sticks, crayons, writing paper, and pencils.

Directions

1 Reread the poem "My Game" as a class. Then point out the list of prepositions on the board. Explain that these words help tell where things are located.

2 Next, invite children to use prepositions to describe the position of objects in the classroom. Elicit responses with questions such as: *Where is the bulletin board?* (next to the door); *Where is the clock?* (over the desk); *Where are your coats?* (in the cubbies); and so on.

3 Then invite children to use the art materials to design their very own room. They can cut pictures of objects from magazines and paste them on construction paper. Children can also draw their own objects with crayons. As they work, encourage children to think about the position of objects in relationship to other objects in the room.

4 Once the room designs are complete, have children write prepositional phrases near the objects, such as *over the fireplace, on the wall,* and *beside the chair.*

5 Older children might write a summary paragraph describing their room on a separate sheet of paper. Encourage them to use prepositional phrases in their descriptions.

What Am I?

Objective

❂ to use sight words in prepositional phrases

❂ to guess classroom objects based on location

Setup

On index cards, write the names of classroom objects, such as *clock*, *pencil sharpener*, *door*, *window*, *teacher's desk*, and *sharing chair*. Create at least one card per child. Place the cards in a hat, bag, or box.

Directions

1. Explain to children that they will be playing a guessing game to practice using prepositions. Show children the hat, bag, or box and tell them it contains cards with the names of "secret" classroom objects.

2. Have a child randomly pick a card and give the class one clue about the object on his or her card. The clue can relate to the object's color, size, shape, or use.

3. Then have children ask questions that contain prepositional phrases to help them guess the item. For instance, questions might include: *Is it near the door? Is it on the bookshelf? Is it on top of the desk?* The clue-giver can answer "warm" or "cool," depending on how close the secret item is to that location.

4. When children think they know the item, have them raise their hands and call out their guesses. If the item is guessed correctly, another volunteer selects the next card. If not, children continue asking questions until the item is revealed.

Sight Word Focus

Prepositions

MATERIALS

○ index cards

○ marker

○ hat, bag, or box

Two Funny, Little Red Apples

Two funny, little red apples
Fell from a tree one day.
Both small apples rolled and rolled
Till they got far away.

They rolled into a **big, green** yard,
Right past **three white** dogs.
They rolled right past a **cold, blue**
lake, And over **four brown** logs.

They didn't stop. They kept on going,
Fast as a speeding train.
Until they felt some **small,** wet drops
Fall from the dark sky as rain.

They rolled into a **pretty, new** house,
Where a **kind** lady made them dry.
Then she put the **two clean, red**
apples into her apple pie!

Perfect Poems for Teaching Sight Words Scholastic Teaching Resources

Using the Poem

Write the poem "Two Funny, Little Red Apples," on chart paper, highlighting the adjectives with a different color marker. First, read the poem to children, pointing to the words as you go. Then divide the class into pairs. Have children reread the poem line by line, letting each pair read a different line. (For step-by-step instructions on sharing the poems, see pages 8–9.) Then point out the highlighted words to children. Explain that these words are *adjectives*—words that describe people, places, or things.

Activity 1

Describe It

Objectives

🌸 to understand that adjectives are describing words

🌸 to identify sight word adjectives in the poem

🌸 to brainstorm adjectives to describe a picture

Setup

🌸 Display the chart paper poem you created for "Two Funny, Little Red Apples" (see Using the Poem, above). Underline each noun in the poem using a different-colored marker than the adjectives.

🌸 Cut out pictures from magazines featuring people, animals, places, and things. Choose pictures with multiple elements that will easily elicit nouns and adjectives, such as a circus advertisement featuring a *huge* elephant and a *funny* clown.

Sight Word Focus

Adjectives

MATERIALS

○ colored markers

○ pictures cut from magazines

Directions

1. Remind children that the highlighted words are describing words, or *adjectives*. Then draw their attention to the underlined words. Explain that they are *nouns* and that a noun names a person, animal, place, thing, or idea.

2. Next, show children one of the magazine pictures. Ask what they see and list their responses in a column on the right side of the chalkboard under the heading *Nouns*. Then invite children to describe each noun with one or more adjectives. For instance, a *dog* might be *brown* and *furry* and a *flower* might be *purple* and *pretty*. Use a different color marker to list children's adjectives on the left side of the chalkboard under the heading *Adjectives*, across from the corresponding nouns.

3. Next, divide the class into pairs and provide each pair with a different magazine picture and a sheet of writing paper. Have children fold their papers lengthwise, then unfold to create two columns. They can then follow the example from the board, with their own nouns and adjectives.

Match and Draw

Sight Word Focus

Adjectives

MATERIALS

- 56 index cards
- two paper bags
- drawing paper
- crayons and/or markers
- pushpins

Objectives

- to illustrate adjective-noun phrases using sight words
- to match adjective-noun phrases to drawings

Setup

- On 28 index cards, write the following nouns: *baby, ball, bed, boat, boy, cake, car, chair, corn, doll, farm, feet, flower, girl, grass, head, hill, nest, picture, seed, shoe, song, street, table, toy, tree, watch* and *window*. Place the cards in a paper bag labeled "Nouns."

- On 28 index cards, write the following adjectives: *big, black, blue, brown, clean, cold, eight, fast, first, five, four, funny, green, hot, little, long, many, new, one, pretty, red, round, small, three, two, warm, white,* and *yellow.* Place the cards in a separate paper bag labeled "Adjectives."

Directions

1 Have each child randomly draw one card from each bag and put them together to create an adjective-noun phrase (*brown table, yellow flower,* and so on). If children pick a numerical adjective, show them how to make their noun plural (*five toys, four nests*).

2 Provide children with paper, markers, and crayons and invite them to draw a picture that illustrates their phrase. Encourage children to be creative: a *cold tree* might be covered in icicles, and a *fast chair* might have wheels! (If children choose a particularly difficult combination, allow them to pick new cards.)

3 When children are finished, post their illustrations on a bulletin board. Post or lay out the nouns and adjectives nearby, in mixed-up order.

4 Then let the matching begin! Encourage the group to work together to find the two cards that go with each picture and post them beneath the corresponding illustration.

5 Once all the words and pictures have been matched, leave the completed display up in the classroom for sight word reading practice.

Double Silly

I have a **funny little kitty**
Who jumps **off** of me.
In **all** the red and **yellow** flowers
She tries to catch a bee.

My brother has a **pretty rabbit**
That he likes to **carry**.
In the **fall**, we play base**ball**,
And eat **small apples** and berries.

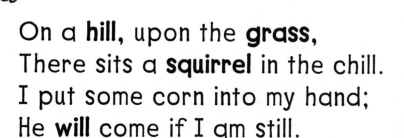

On a **hill**, upon the **grass**,
There sits a **squirrel** in the chill.
I put some corn into my hand;
He **will** come if I am still.

I **shall** write a **letter** to my **doll**
If the weather does not get **better**.
I **will tell** her to keep **well**,
And to **pull** on her warm sweater!

Using the Poem

Write the poem "Double Silly" on chart paper, using a different-colored marker for the highlighted same double-consonant words. After reading the poem together, draw children's attention to the highlighted words and ask them what they notice. Point out the double consonants and ask children if they can think of any other examples of these kinds of words (*happy*, *balloon*, and so on). For tips on how to share the poems, see pages 8–9.

see pages 8–9.

Sight Word Focus

Same Double-Consonant Words

MATERIALS

- index cards
- hat, bag, or box
- pencils or markers
- sentence strips

Activity 1

Missing Doubles

Objectives

- to place appropriate double consonants in sight words
- to use double-consonant sight words in sentences

Setup

Write each of the following double-consonant words (with blanks for the boldface missing letters) on an index card: squi**rr**el, le**tt**er, fu**nn**y, ye**ll**ow, pre**tt**y, li**tt**le, be**tt**er, ca**rr**y, ra**bb**it, ki**tt**y, we**ll**, sha**ll**, do**ll**, hi**ll**, a**pp**le, ba**ll**, pu**ll**, te**ll**, fa**ll**, sma**ll**, o**ff**, a**ll**. Place the cards in a hat, bag, or box.

Directions

1. Divide the class into pairs. Have each pair pick a card from the hat, bag, or box. Let pairs work together to decide which double-consonant pair is missing.

2. Next, have children write the completed word, and then a sentence using that word, on a sentence strip. (Be sure children do not write on the original word card.)

3. When each pair is finished, have children present the original word card to the class. Invite volunteers to guess the missing letters, say the complete word, and then read aloud the sentence on the strip.

Double Fun

Objectives

❀ to write and illustrate sentences using several double-consonant sight words

Setup

Write the double-consonant words from Activity 1 on the chalkboard (see page 62). Provide each child with a sheet of paper, a pencil, and crayons or markers.

Directions

1 Read the list of double-consonant words aloud with children.

2 Invite children to create a sentence using as many of the double-consonant words as they can—for instance: *The funny squirrel shared a small apple with the pretty rabbit.* (If they like, children can also include their own double-consonant words, such as *butter, fiddle,* or *teddy bear.*)

3 Have children write their sentences on the bottom (lined) part of the paper and draw a corresponding picture on the top (blank) section.

4 Let children share their sentences and illustrations with the class. You can display their work on a bulletin board, or bind the pages together to create a class book entitled "Double Fun"!

MATERIALS

○ paper for writing and drawing (lined on the bottom, blank on top)

○ pencils

○ crayons or markers

Terrific Tongue Twisters

Tongue twisters twist your tongue.
It goes this way and that.
Tongue twisters twist your tongue.
Can you imagine that?

Listen for the sound you hear
At the start of almost every word.
Then create your own tongue twister,
And we'll listen for the sound that's heard!

- **Big brown bears buy bread** in a **blue box.**
- Carrie **can cut** and **clean cold corn.**
- Fanny **found five fast** and **funny flies.**
- **He has helped her hold her hurt hand.**
- Lenny **likes** to **laugh** and **live** a **little.**
- **My mother,** May, **made me make** it **myself.**
- **Six sad sheep sleep.**
- **Which window** shall **we wash?**

Perfect Poems for Teaching Sight Words Scholastic Teaching Resources

Using the Poem

Write the poem "Terrific Tongue Twisters" on chart paper, using a different-colored marker for the same initial consonant tongue twister words. Share the poem with children (for step-by-step instructions on sharing poems, see pages 8–9). Then discuss what tongue twisters are. Ask children to think about strategies for reading tongue twisters, such as reading slower, reading to yourself first, or reading aloud to a partner. You might pair children up and assign each pair a different tongue twister from the poem to practice together. You can also invite volunteers to read a tongue twister to the class.

Activity 1

Tongue Twister Towns

Objectives

- to identify the initial consonant sound repeated in tongue twisters containing sight words
- to create and illustrate original tongue twisters

Setup

Display the chart paper poem you created for "Terrific Tongue Twisters" (see Using the Poem, above). Write each of the following consonants on separate small slips of paper: *b, c, d, f, g, h, j, k, l, m, n, p, r, s, t, v,* and *w.* Place the slips of paper in a hat, bag, or box.

Directions

1 Read the poem chart aloud together. Invite children to identify the repeated initial consonant sound in each of the eight tongue twisters. Have volunteers underline the repeated initial letters for each tongue twister on the chart.

2 Next, divide the class into pairs and invite each pair to pick a letter from the hat, bag, or box. Provide pairs with drawing paper, pencils, and crayons or markers.

3 Challenge children to create a "tongue twister town" using the letter they chose. Children can draw and label things in a scene on their paper that begin with that letter. For example, in "Y-Town," you might find *yodeling yams, yelling yaks, yellow yolks,* and *yummy yogurt.* A children's picture dictionary might spark ideas.

Sight Word Focus

Same Beginning
Sound Words

MATERIALS

- small slips of paper
- hat, bag, or box
- drawing paper
- pencils
- crayons and markers

Tongue Twister Tales

Objective

❀ to create cooperative oral stories using same initial consonant words

Setup

Place chairs in a circle or have children sit in a circle on the floor.

Directions

1 Explain that children will work together to create their own tongue twister tale. Each child will add one word to the tale. The trick is, each word must begin with the same sound!

2 Begin the tongue twister yourself by saying a proper name, such as *Suzy*. Then have the child to your left add one word to continue the tongue twister. The next child adds the next word, and so on. (Children can add connecting words such as *to*, *and*, *the*, and *of*.) For example:

> Teacher: Suzy
> Child 1: sold
> Child 2: silly
> Child 3: stamps
> Child 4: to sailors
> Child 5: sitting
> Child 6: by the sea.

3 Continue around the circle until the story comes to a conclusion.

4 Begin a new tongue twister by saying a name with a different initial consonant sound.

Activity 3

Tangled Tongue Twisters

Objective

◆ to use syntactic and semantic cues to unscramble tongue twisters

Setup

◆ Copy the Tangled Tongue Twisters reproducible on page 68 onto heavy paper. (The number of copies you will need depends on your class size: You'll need one tongue twister strip for each pair of children.)

◆ Cut apart the tongue twister strips along the solid lines. Then cut apart the words for each twister, along the dotted lines. Place the word cards for each tongue twister in separate plastic bags.

Directions

1 Divide the class into pairs. Provide each pair with a tongue twister puzzle bag, writing paper, and pencils.

2 Have children open their bags and spread the word cards out on a table. Encourage them to move the cards around until they have a tongue twister that makes sense. As pairs unscramble their tongue twisters, have children write them down (in the correct word order).

3 When pairs are finished, have them put the word cards back in the bag and exchange with another pair. As they unscramble the new twister, have them record it on their paper beneath the first one.

4 Pairs continue to trade puzzle bags until each pair has unscrambled several tangled tongue twisters.

5 When children are finished, have them share their unscrambled tongue twisters aloud. As a class, discuss any similarities and differences among children's interpretations.

Sight Word Focus

Same Beginning
Sound Words

MATERIALS

○ copies of page 68

○ self-sealing bags (one per pair of children)

○ scissors

○ paper

○ pencils

Tangled Tongue Twisters				
bring	Bert's	baby	bird	back
Bob	better	buy	brown	bread
Connie	can	cut	clean	corn
Don	doesn't	dry	dog	dishes
Fred	found	five	full	fish
Father's	feet	feel	fairly	funny
farmers	farm	five	full	fields
Harry	helped	her	hop	home
little	Lily	likes	live	lizards
Mother	made	me	my	milk
Pat	painted	paper	pigs	pink

Tangled Tongue Twisters

bring	Bert's	baby	bird	back
Bob	better	buy	brown	bread
Connie	can	cut	clean	corn
Don	doesn't	dry	dog	dishes
Fred	found	five	full	fish
Father's	feet	feel	fairly	funny
farmers	farm	five	full	fields
Harry	helped	her	hop	home
little	Lily	likes	live	lizards
Mother	made	me	my	milk
Pat	painted	paper	pigs	pink

68

What Am I?

I can roll downhill,
Or lay flat on your dish.
I come from a chicken.
You can scramble me if you wish!
What am I?

I'm needed everywhere.
I begin with small drops.
In dry deserts I am rare,
But I am very good for crops!
What am I?

I wrote it, I stamped it,
I sent it on its way.
I heard it was a big hit
At your birthday party today!
What am I?

I'm a home up high,
And I hold eggs.
You'll find me in trees.
Now take a guess, please!
What am I?

I'm always with you,
I'm attached to your wrist.
I can wave with one, clap with two,
Or make a tight fist!
What am I?

Answers: egg, rain, letter, nest, hand

Perfect Poems for Teaching Sight Words Scholastic Teaching Resources

Using the Poem

Sight Word Focus

Dolch Nouns

MATERIALS

○ pencil and paper
○ sticky notes

Activity 1

Solving Riddles

Objectives

❋ to find Dolch words that help solve riddles

❋ to explain solutions to riddles

Setup

Display the chart paper poem you created for "What Am I?," making sure a sticky note covers each answer word (see Using the Poem, above).

Directions

1 Ask children: *What is a riddle?* Explain that a riddle is like a question. Reread the riddle poem with children.

2 One riddle at a time, encourage children to find clue words that might help them guess the answer. For instance, clue words for the first riddle might include *roll*, *chicken*, and *scramble*; clues to the third riddle might include *stamped*, *sent*, and *birthday*.

3 After finding the clue words, invite children to guess the answer to each riddle. You can then remove the sticky notes to let children check their guesses and read the sight words.

4 Children can write their own riddles (they do not need to rhyme). If you like, brainstorm a list of themes as a class (animals, holidays, food, colors, numbers, places, and so on). Remind children to use clue words in their riddles. Then let children share their riddles for others to guess.

Perfect Poems for Teaching Sight Words Scholastic Teaching Resources

Hink Pinks

Objective

❋ to read sight words that are nouns and adjectives

❋ to write original "hink pink" riddles and build awareness of sight words that rhyme

Setup

Write the following hink pinks on sentence strips. Write each answer on the reverse side of the strip.

❋ *What is a hink pink for a large hog?* (big pig)

❋ *What is a hink pink for a chubby kitty?* (fat cat)

❋ *What is a hink pink for an unhappy father?* (sad dad)

Directions

1 Explain that a hink pink is a riddle whose answer consists of two one-syllable words that rhyme.

2 Present the prepared hink pink sentence strips. Help children solve each hink pink by inviting them to think of synonyms for each clue word. For instance, for the first hink pink, ask: *What other words can you think of that mean the same as* large? Once children guess the first word correctly (*big*), invite them to think of a rhyming synonym for *hog* (*pig*). When children solve each riddle, turn the sentence strip over to reveal the answer.

3 Once children are familiar with the concept, invite them to work in pairs to write their own hink pink riddles. You might encourage children to work backward: They can start by coming up with the rhyming two-word answer, and then think of synonyms to use for their question. When pairs are finished, have them present their hink pinks for the class to solve.

4 As an extension activity, you can have children write hinky pinkies: riddles whose answers consist of two two-syllable rhyming words. For example: *What is a hinky pinky for a silly rabbit?* (Answer: *funny bunny*)

Sight Word Focus

Dolch Nouns and Adjectives

MATERIALS

○ sentence strips

○ writing paper

○ pencils

Who Am I?

Objective

❋ to use clue words to create riddles about classmates

Setup

❋ On chart paper, write the following riddle:

> *I work in a special place at school.*
> *I show you how to find a good book.*
> *I help you find information.*
> *I can read you stories and poems.*
> *Who am I?*

❋ Set aside one hat, bag, or box for children's riddles.

❋ Place the slips of paper with children's names inside the second hat, bag, or box.

Directions

1 Introduce the prepared chart paper riddle. Discuss each of the four clues together and invite children to guess the answer (*librarian*).

2 Next, invite each child to create his or her own riddle, following the example by writing four clues about him- or herself and ending with the phrase *Who am I?* (Younger children can dictate their clues.) Children's clues might relate to favorite activities, hair color, eye color, clothes they are wearing that day, and so on. Make sure children do not write their names on their riddles. Place riddles in a hat, bag, or box.

3 Have each child randomly pick a riddle and read the clues aloud to the class. When the group guesses the child the riddle is about, the child who wrote it can stand up to confirm the answer. Continue until all children are standing.

4 Children can also write riddles about their classmates. Let each child choose a name from the hat, bag, or box and create a riddle about that person, following the same format. Let children share their riddles with the class as the group guesses the answers.

Sight Word Focus

Dolch Nouns

MATERIALS

○ chart paper

○ writing paper

○ pencils

○ two hats, bags, or boxes

○ small slips of paper printed with children's names (one per child)

Clap Your Hands

Say each word.
Hear each sound.
Clap your hands
For each one found.

Red, for, big, and **blue.**
Clap just once,
And then you're through.

Look, make, go, and **please.**
Each has one syllable.
Now try these!

Going, myself, and **today.**
You clap twice
For each sound you say.

Over, under, and **before.**
Each has two syllables.
Can you think of any more?

Using the Poem

Write the poem "Clap Your Hands" on chart paper, using a different-colored marker for the highlighted words. You may want to use one color for one-syllable words and a different color for two-syllable words. Read the poem with children (for more tips on sharing poems, see pages 8–9).

Sight Word Focus

Counting Syllables

MATERIALS

- 30 large index cards
- small index cards (one per child)

Activity 1

Syllable Signal

Objective

❋ to distinguish between one- and two-syllable sight words

Setup

❋ Display the chart paper poem you created for "Clap Your Hands" (see Using the Poem, above).

❋ Print one of the following sight words on each of the large index cards: *see, clean, draw, drink, grow, laugh, start, keep, full, thank, round, sing, jump, help, long, about, better, carry, myself, today, never, after, going, because, before, over, away, funny, little, under.* On each small index card, write the numeral 1 on one side and the numeral 2 on the other. Distribute a card to each child.

Directions

1. Begin by rereading the poem to children. As you read, model how to clap your hands once on the highlighted one-syllable words and twice on the highlighted two-syllable words.

2. Then read the poem again, this time inviting children to clap out the syllables in the highlighted words.

3. Next, have children take out their numeral cards. Explain that you will be showing children sight words that have both one and two syllables. As you hold up each word card and read it aloud, have children hold up the side of their card that shows the number of syllables they hear. For example, children would hold up the 1 side for the word *see* and the 2 side for the word *funny*.

4. Continue until the group has clapped out each word.

Activity 2

Syllable Sort

Objectives

🌀 to sort sight words by the number of syllables they contain

🌀 to write sight words that contain one and two syllables

Setup

🌀 Divide the class into groups of several children each. For each group, prepare a set of 20 index cards by printing a different sight word on each. Include both one- and two-syllable words, and vary the words as much as possible from set to set. (See the Dolch lists on pages 10–12 for word choices.)

🌀 Distribute a set of prepared cards to each group, along with pencils and five blank index cards.

Directions

1 Invite each group to work together to read the words on their cards. Encourage volunteers to take turns reading the words aloud as group members clap out the syllables.

2 Next, have children sort their cards into two piles, according to the number of syllables they contain (one or two).

3 On the blank cards, have children write five new words (they might like to use classmates' names). Explain that each word or name should contain either one or two syllables. Then have children sort their new cards into the appropriate piles.

4 When groups are finished, have them mix up all 25 cards and then exchange with another group to repeat the activity.

Sight Word Focus

Counting Syllables

MATERIALS

○ 25 index cards per small group of children

○ pencils

Syllable Add-Ons

Sight Word Focus

Counting Syllables

MATERIALS

○ index cards

○ magnets or magnetic tape

Objectives

❖ to attach common suffixes to one-syllable sight words

❖ to create sentences using the new words

Setup

❖ Write one of the following suffixes on each of five index cards: *-ing, -er, -ful, -est,* and *-able.* Attach a piece of magnetic tape to the back of each card and place the cards in a row on the chalkboard. Or, use regular magnets to post the cards.

❖ Beneath the cards, list the following sight words on the board: *see, full, thank, light, drink, keep, new, hurt, cold, walk, start, long, help, round, laugh, grow, kind, hurt, big, wash, clean, small, watch, hot,* and *jump.*

Directions

1 Point out the suffix index cards and ask: *Where are these word parts usually found?* (at the ends of words) Tell children that these word endings are called suffixes. Together, count out the number of syllables in each suffix.

2 Invite children to take turns coming to the board to create new words. They can do this by attaching one of the suffix cards to the end of one of the sight words. Help children read the word aloud, both before and after attaching the suffix. Does it make a real word?

3 Before returning the suffix card to its place at the top of the board, help children use chalk to write the word ending on the board next to the original word. Be sure to point out necessary spelling changes in words such as *hottest* and *biggest* (an extra letter is added to correctly spell the new word).

4 Once children have completed the new word, have them count out the number of syllables and then challenge them to use the new word in a sentence.

5 Continue until each sight word has been given a suffix.

Word Families

We all belong to a family.
We all belong to a group.
We all belong to a family,
A class, a team, or troop.

A word can belong to a family
Of words with the same look and sound.
Like hit, bit, **sit**, and fit,
Or found, **round**, and **ground**.

Bake, **cake**, and rake are in a family.
So are hop, mop, and drop.
Which words belong to the same family
As flop, crop, and **stop**?

Which words belong to the families
Of **play** and **can** and **ball**?
Which words belong in the family of **got**?
Let's try to name them all!

Using the Poem

Write the poem "Word Families" on chart paper, using different colored-markers for the highlighted words (you may want to use a separate color for each word family). Read the poem aloud to children. Then divide the class into two groups and have groups alternate lines. Next, have groups alternate every two lines. Finally, have groups alternate stanzas. To wrap up, have the whole class read the entire poem together. For tips on sharing the poem, see pages 8–9.

Sight Word Focus

Word Family Words

MATERIALS

- nine sheets chart paper
- markers

Activity 1

Word Family Race

Objective

- to brainstorm Dolch and non-Dolch words that belong to the following word families: -it, -ound, -ake, -op, -ay, -an, -all, -ot, and -at
- to create a Word Family Word Wall in the classroom

Setup

At the top of each sheet of chart paper, write one of the following rimes from the poem: -it, -ound, -ake, -op, -ay, -an, -all, -ot, or -at.

Directions

1 After reading the poem (see Using the Poem, above), discuss the concept of word families with children. Point out that word family words not only sound alike (rhyme) but also end with the same spelling pattern.

2 Divide the class into nine teams. Give each team a sheet of chart paper (with a rime printed at the top) and a marker. Explain that teams will have five minutes to write as many word family words for their word ending as they can. When you say "Go," have children record the words on the paper.

3 When the five minutes are up, have teams share their words with the class.

4 Have children print the words on individual index cards. Post these cards on separate sections of a bulletin board (one section per family) to begin a Word Family Word Wall. You can expand on this wall as described in Activity 2 (see page 79).

Word Family Wall

Sight Word Focus

Word Family Words

Objectives

🌸 to identify and write Dolch and non-Dolch words belonging to various word families

🌸 to sort and categorize words belonging to various word families

🌸 to create a Word Family Word Wall in the classroom

Setup

🌸 Print the following rimes on index cards (since you will need four cards per child, each rime will be used more than once):

-ab	-eat	-ice	-ob	-un
-ace	-ed	-ig	-og	-um
-ack	-eep	-ight	-old	-ub
-age	-en	-ill	-oy	-ust
-am	-est	-in	-ope	-ush

🌸 Place the completed cards in a hat, bag, or box.

MATERIALS

○ index cards (four per child)

○ hat, bag, or box

○ markers

Directions

1 Have each child pick four index cards from the hat, bag, or box.

2 Invite children to add a letter or letters at the beginning of the rime to create a new word. Encourage children to try to create words they think no one else in the class will think of.

3 When children are finished, invite them to share their words and compare them to the words of other children who chose the same rime. These children might stand in front of the group and hold up their cards.

4 Then draw children's attention to the Word Family Word Wall you began in Activity 1 (see page 78). Have children expand the word wall by adding their new words to different sections of the bulletin board.

Word Family Flip Books

Sight Word Focus

Word Family Words

MATERIALS

○ 8 1/2- by 11-inch paper (one sheet per child)

○ 8 1/2- by 2-inch strips of paper (one per child)

○ stapler

○ small slips of paper

○ hat, bag, or box

○ pencils

○ markers or crayons

Objectives

❋ to create word family books of Dolch and non-Dolch words by adding initial letter(s) to rimes

❋ to illustrate the new words

Setup

❋ In advance, as a model for children, make a flip book as follows. First, cut an 8 1/2- by 11-inch sheet of paper into 10 equal pieces (approximately 2 by 4 inches each). Stack the 10 small pieces and then attach a 2- by 8 1/2-inch strip of paper to the back. Staple together in the upper left corner (see below right).

❋ Write the word family rimes used in Activity 1 (page 78) and Activity 2 (page 79) on small slips of paper. Place the slips in a hat, bag, or box.

Directions

1 Help children prepare blank flip books and staple them. Then have each child randomly pick a rime from the hat, bag, or box.

2 To begin the flip book, have the child write his or her rime on the right side of the long strip of paper, next to the smaller pages.

3 Then, on each of the 10 small flip book sheets, invite children to write a different initial letter or letters that will form a word with the rime. For instance, if a child writes *ake* on the long strip, he or she might write *c*, *r*, and *sn* on the small pages to form the words *cake*, *rake*, and *snake*. (If children have trouble coming up with 10 words, they can confer with classmates for additional ideas. For older children, a rhyming dictionary is also a good resource.)

4 On the back of each letter square, children can illustrate the word.

5 When children are finished, let them trade books and have fun flipping the pages to see new words.

One Word Out

Some words belong together
Because they are alike.
Words like seat, wheels, and pedals
Are all parts of my bike.

Big, large, and huge
Are words that mean the same.
Tag, jump rope, and hopscotch
Are all kinds of fun games.

Let's see if you can choose
The word that does not fit
In each group of words below:
Just find and circle it!

1.	yellow	blue	four	red
2.	I	me	your	my
3.	warm	cold	many	hot
4.	down	seven	six	eight
5.	run	walk	jump	laugh
6.	to	blue	two	too
7.	say	play	over	may

Using the Poem

Sight Word Focus

Word Categories

MATERIALS

○ marker

Activity 1

Which Word Out?

Objectives

❁ to identify the word that does not belong in a given group of sight words

❁ to state similarities and differences among given words

Setup

Display the chart paper poem you created for "One Word Out" (see Using the Poem, above).

Directions

1 After reading the poem "One Word Out" with children, call their attention to the seven sets of words.

2 Ask a volunteer to come up to the chart and read aloud the first group of words. Have that child choose the word he or she thinks does not belong and tell why. Invite the class to signal agreement with a thumbs-up. Once the class has agreed which word does not belong, have the volunteer circle it with a marker. (See below for correct answers.)

3 Repeat for each of the remaining word sets.

Answers

1. *four* is the only word that is not a color

2. *your* is the only word that refers to someone else

3. *many* is the only word that does not refer to temperature

4. *down* is the only word that is not a number

5. *laugh* is the only activity not done with the legs and feet

6. *blue* is the only word that sounds different when read aloud

7. *over* is the only word that is not part of the word family

Activity 2

Brainstorm!

Objective

❁ to state sight words that belong to a specific category

Setup

Print names of several word categories on separate index cards. Also have available blank index cards for categories children may suggest. Categories might include:

songs	*farm animals*
fruit	*colors*
vegetables	*things found in school*
clothing	*holidays*
jobs	*playground games*
things you ride	*weather words*

Directions

1 Have a volunteer choose a category card and read it aloud to the class.

2 Invite the group to brainstorm words that fit the category. Children can raise their hands each time they come up with a new word. For instance, words for the weather category might include *hot, cold, storm,* and *rain.*

3 Record the words on chart paper. Continue until children run out of words for the category.

4 Repeat with a different category.

Magazine Scavenger Hunt Collage

MATERIALS

- large sheets of plain construction paper
- scissors
- glue sticks
- old magazines
- sticky notes

Objectives

❧ to locate Dolch and non-Dolch words and pictures that belong to a specific category

Setup

Provide children with large sheets of construction paper, scissors, glue sticks, old magazines, and sticky notes.

Directions

1 Invite each child to choose a category for his or her collage. You might like to brainstorm possible categories as a class (foods, feelings, sports, and so on). You can also let children choose from categories not used in Activity 2 (see page 83).

2 Invite children to write the names of their categories in the center of their papers. Then have them go on a scavenger hunt through old magazines to find words and pictures that fit the category. For instance, a child who chose sports might glue on pictures of equipment and athletes, and words such as *baseball* and *score*.

3 Encourage children to share any words and pictures they find that another classmate might be able to use. For instance, a child who is creating a sports collage might find a picture of an apple and give it to a child creating a collage of fruits.

4 Have children glue down their pictures, and help them label each of them with a sticky note.

I Have a Little Secret

I have a little secret.
Look inside the word **before**.
Can you find some little words?
Like **be** and **for** and **or**?

I want to be a detective
In a near or far-off land,
But for now I'll just search words
To find **an** and **and** in **hand**.

In **sit**, there's **it**.
There's **let** in **letter**.
In **chair**, there's air.
Find a word in **together**!

In **stop**, there's **top**.
In **start**, find art.
What words are in **think**?
Oh, you're so smart.

Find many little words in this:
The **funny, yellow party cat**
Ran around the **flower bed**
And sat with robin **for** a chat.

Now you know my little secret.
Think of big words like I do.
Look for little words in big ones.
Each letter is a clue!

Using the Poem

Children love secrets and mysteries, and this poem has both! Write the poem "I Have a Little Secret" on chart paper, using a different-colored marker for the highlighted words. Try using one color for the "big" words (*before, hand, sit, letter, chair, together, stop, start, think*, and each highlighted word in the fifth stanza) and another color for the "little" words (*be, for, or, an, and, it, let, air, top, art*). Then read the poem aloud to children (for step-by-step instructions on sharing poems, see pages 8–9). Ask: *What is the secret in the poem? What does a "word detective" do?* To help children start solving the "word mysteries," see Activity 1 below.

see pages 8–9

Sight Word Focus

Words Within Words

MATERIALS

○ copies of page 87 (one for every two children)

○ chart paper

○ markers

Activity 1

Word Spy

Objective

❁ to locate and identify small sight words within larger words

Setup

❁ Display the chart paper poem you created for "I Have a Little Secret" (see Using the Poem, above).

❁ Post another sheet of chart paper next to the poem. Across the top, write the heading *Word Detectives at Work*. Then draw a line down the middle to create two columns. Label the first column *Words Are Hiding Here!* and the second column *Words We Found*.

Directions

1 After reading the poem with children, explain that they will be "word detectives." Their job is to find "secret" small words in larger words.

2 Invite children to point out the larger highlighted words in the poem that need to be "investigated" (*together, start, think*, and the highlighted words in the fifth stanza). Write these words on the chart paper in the *Words Are Hiding Here!* column.

3 Next, let children play Word Spy. Give each child a Word Spy sheet and invite him or her to choose a word from the list. They write this word on the first line, then record any words they can find within. Together, in the second column, list the words children found.

Perfect Poems for Teaching Sight Words Scholastic Teaching Resources

Word Spy

There are some words hiding in this word:

_____

Here they are!

_____   _____

_____   _____

Word Spy

There are some words hiding in this word:

_____

Here they are!

_____   _____

_____   _____

String Bean Word Soup

Objectives

✦ to find small sight words in larger words

Setup

✦ Copy the string bean patterns (page 89) and distribute one to each child. Have children cut apart the string bean patterns so that they have a pile of string beans. Then have children place them in a cup or bowl beside their bowl-shaped (semicircle) sheet of construction paper.

Directions

1 Begin by telling children that they will be "cooking" a pot of string bean soup. The problem is, the beans are too long! Explain that children will need to look at the word on each bean to find the right place to "snap" it into smaller pieces.

2 Invite children to pick a string bean from their cup or bowl and read the word. Can they find one or more smaller words on the bean? Have children cut the bean into pieces to create the new word(s) and then glue them onto their paper "bowls." For instance, a bean with the word *upon* can be cut into two pieces: *up* and *on*.

3 As children continue choosing and cutting beans, explain that any letters that cannot be used may be put aside. For example, *window* can be cut to make *win* and *do*; the final *w* can be set aside and used to form a new word. Children may find yet another small word in a bean that has already been cut (*shall* can be cut to *hall*, which contains *all*). In this case, have children circle the smaller word on the cut bean.

4 When children are finished, have them "read" their soup words to a friend. They can also write other words that contain smaller words on the blank beans.

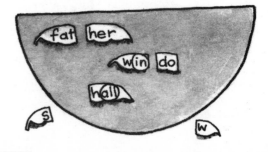

Sight Word Focus

Words Within Words

MATERIALS

○ copies of page 89 (one per child)

○ scissors

○ small paper cups or bowls (one per child)

○ construction paper cut into semicircles (one per child)

○ glue sticks

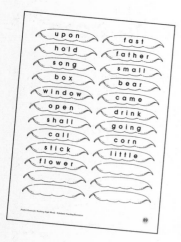

upon

hold

song

box

window

open

shall

call

stick

flower

fast

father

small

bear

came

drink

going

corn

little

Mystery Sentences

Sight Word Focus

Words Within Words

MATERIALS

○ copies of page 91 (one per child)

○ pencils

Objective

❀ to find small sight words in larger words

❀ to logically complete sentences

Setup

❀ Write the following "mystery sentence" on the chalkboard: "Johnny, call _____ the dogs into the house."

❀ Copy the Mystery Sentences reproducible (page 91) and distribute one to each child.

Directions

1 Begin by working through the example on the board with children. First, read the sentence aloud. Then encourage children to look carefully at each word. Can children find a smaller, "hidden" word that will complete the sentence?

2 Point out the word *call* and ask, *What smaller word do you see in this word?* (all) Circle the word *all* in *call* and ask, *Does this word complete the sentence?* (yes)

3 Write the word *all* on the line and then read the completed sentence aloud with children.

4 When children are familiar with the process, encourage them to use the same method to complete the Mystery Sentences on their sheets. Depending on children's level, you may want to work through a few more sentences as a group, or pair children up for the activity.

5 When children are finished, let them exchange papers and compare answers.

Answers: 1. *farm* in *farmer*; 2. *ink* in *drink*; 3. *or* in *door*; 4. *hat* in *what*; 5. *row* in *grow*; 6. *how* in *show*; 7. *ring* in *bring*; 8. *able* in *table*; 9. *ouch* in *couch*.

Mystery Sentences

Read each sentence. Look carefully at the boldface word to find a hidden word that will complete the sentence. Circle the hidden word. Then write it on the line.

1. The **farmer** has work to do on his _____.

2. Never **drink** _____!

3. Should we open the window _____ open the **door**?

4. **What** kind of _____ will you wear on your head?

5. I will **grow** a _____ of corn.

6. I do not know _____ we will get to the **show**.

7. Our teacher **brings** us to class when the bell _____.

8. Please set the **table** if you are _____.

9. I fell off the **couch** and yelled, "_____!"

May, Bea, Ike, Joe, and Beulah

May, Bea, Ike, Joe, and Beulah
Are friends to me and friends to you.
Read and see if you agree
That they are as different as they can be.

May can **play games**
In the **rain** all **day**.
May can **make** great **cakes**
For her best friend, Jay.

Bea **keeps three seeds**
In the deep **green** weeds.
She likes to **clean**,
And **she** likes to **read**.

Ike **likes** to **ride**
On his tiny **white** bike.
Ike **likes** to climb,
And he **likes** to hike.

Joe loves to **go**
Out in the **snow**.
And owns a **boat**
That he likes to row.

Beulah can **use** a tube
Of bright **blue** glue
To fix her bike.
Now her bike won't move!

Perfect Poems for Teaching Sight Words Scholastic Teaching Resources

Using the Poem

The poem "May, Bea, Ike, Joe, and Beulah" combines friends and their interests with long vowel sounds. Write the poem on chart paper, using different colored markers for the highlighted words. Use a separate color to highlight words with the featured long vowel sound in each stanza (for example, write the long-*a* words in the second stanza with a red marker, the long-*e* words in the third stanza with a green marker, and so on). Then read the poem aloud to children. For more tips on sharing poems, see pages 8–9.

Activity 1

Sound Mystery

Sight Word Focus

Words With Long Vowel Sounds

MATERIALS

○ none

Objectives

❧ to identify sight words with long vowel sounds

❧ to use long vowel sound clues to answer questions

Setup

Display the chart paper poem you created for "May, Bea, Ike, Joe, and Beulah" (see Using the Poem, above).

Directions

1 After reading the poem once through with children, read it again line by line. Invite children to do an echo reading by repeating each line after you.

2 Next, help children examine each stanza to discover what is interesting about each of the five friends. Draw attention to the highlighted words and ask, *What sound do you hear in these words?* Lead children to see that each friend likes things that contain the same vowel sound as his or her name. Explain that these are called long vowel sounds. Long vowel sounds sound like the letter name of the vowel.

3 Read each question (see right) aloud, emphasizing the words with long vowel sounds. Explain that the sounds in these words will give children clues to the answer. As children make their guesses, encourage them to tell why they chose that friend.

Long Vowel Questions

1. *Who takes the train?* (May)
2. *Who likes the color white?* (Ike)
3. *Who throws snow?* (Joe)
4. *Who likes unicorns?* (Beulah)
5. *Who needs the number three?* (Bea)
6. *Who do you see in the tree?* (Bea)
7. *Who came on a plane?* (May)
8. *Who uses a night light?* (Ike)
9. *Who loves oranges?* (Joe)

Sweet Sounds

Objectives

* to discriminate among long vowel sounds
* to sort sight words by long vowel sounds
* to write words containing long vowel sounds

Setup

MATERIALS

○ Five copies of
page 95

○ copy of page 96

○ copy of page 97

○ posterboard

○ scissors

○ glue

○ magnetic tape or
pushpins

○ removable adhesive

○ hat, bag, or box

○ pencils

* Make five copies of the cake pattern (page 95). Glue the cake patterns to a sheet of posterboard (for durability) and cut them out. Label each cake with one of the following: *a, e, i, o, u.* You can attach the cakes to the chalkboard with magnetic tape, or use pushpins or removable adhesive to attach them to a bulletin board or wall.

* Make one copy of the blank candle patterns on page 96 and cut them apart.

* Make one copy of the sight word candles on page 97. Cut apart the candles and place them in a hat, bag, or box.

Directions

1. Show children the cakes and read the labels aloud. Explain that children will be putting candles on the birthday cakes according to vowel sounds. Children might like to color the cakes.

2. Have children take turns picking a sight word candle from the hat, bag, or box. The child then reads the word aloud, names the long vowel sound, and attaches the candle to the correct cake with removable adhesive.

3. Continue until all the printed candles have been sorted and placed on the cakes. Next, give each child a blank candle. Invite children to think of a new word that contains a long vowel sound of their choice. (Depending on children's level, you might brainstorm a list of possibilities.) Then have children write the word on their candle, read the word aloud, and place it on the appropriate cake.

4. For an additional challenge, help children examine the words on each cake and identify the different spelling patterns for each long vowel sound.

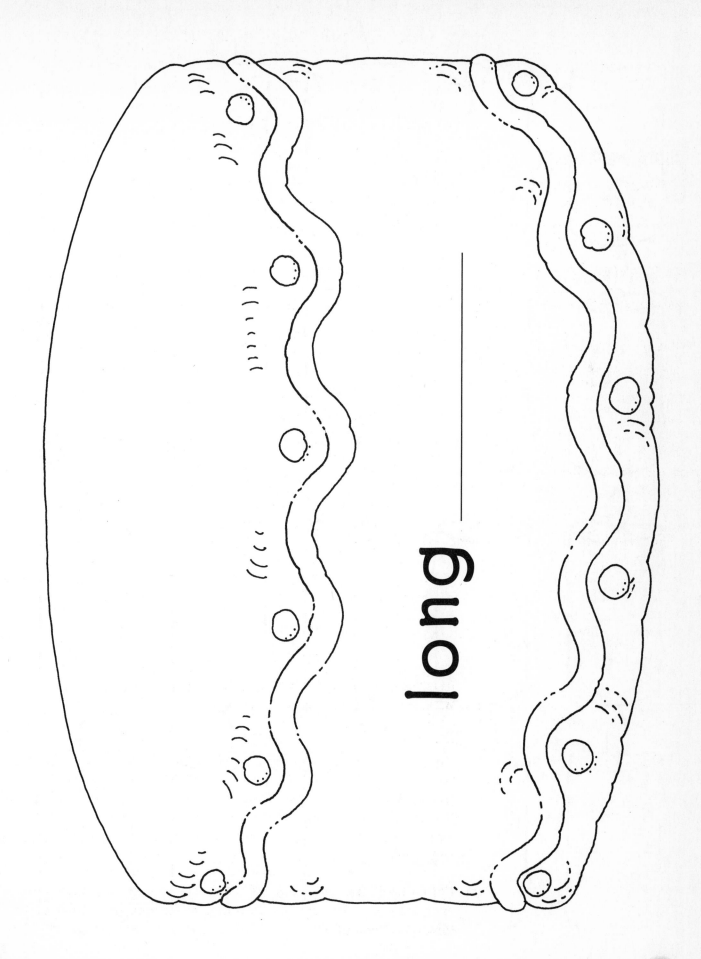

long

96

my three no may sleep few we please eat these

find play ride take those go you say buy use

I ate she five make be so gave clean me

came white green grow eat right made keep light play

he fly read kind own show see like know write

Swat the Word

Objective

- to identify Dolch and non-Dolch words with different long vowel sounds

Setup

On each of the 50 index cards, write one of the long vowel sight words from the candles on page 97. Attach a piece of magnetic tape to the back of each card and attach the cards to the chalkboard randomly. Otherwise, you can simply post the cards on the board using a small piece of tape or regular magnets.

Directions

1. Divide the class into two teams and have each team line up in front of the chalkboard. Give the first child in each line a flyswatter.

2. Call out a long vowel sound, such as long a or long e. Each player tries to find a word with that sound, read it aloud, and swat the word with the swatter (remind children to be careful with their swatters). The first player to successfully read and swat a correct word removes the card from the board.

3. If a player swats an incorrect word, the other player gets a chance to locate, read, swat, and remove another word with the vowel sound.

4. When the first two players have completed the round, have them hand the flyswatter to the next child in line and then get in the back of the line.

5. Continue play, calling out a different vowel sound for each round, until the board is empty. The team with the most cards wins.

Sight Word Focus

Words With Long Vowel Sounds

MATERIALS

- 50 index cards
- magnetic tape or magnets
- two flyswatters

Singing Ducks

Some silly yellow ducks
Sat upon their little nests.
And sang a silly song
To keep away the pests.

One duck sang,
"Robin came to visit me.
It really was so much fun.
We ate eggs and fish,
And laid out in the sun."

One duck sang,
"I shall help the men
Who pick up all the litter
Over and over again
To save every critter."

One duck sang,
"Furry little rabbit,
With your strong legs.
You dash, hop, and flit
Like you're scrambling some eggs!"

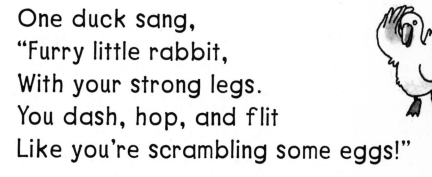

The ducks all sang at once.
They all sang together.
They'll keep singing all year long
In every kind of weather.

Using the Poem

Write the poem "Singing Ducks" on chart paper. If you like, you can use a separate color to highlight words with short vowel sounds. Read the poem once through with children. For tips on sharing poems, see pages 8–9.

Activity 1

Short Vowel Word Wall

Sight Word Focus

Words With Short Vowel Sounds

MATERIALS

○ index cards

○ markers

Objectives

❧ to identify Dolch and non-Dolch words with short vowel sounds

❧ to write words with short vowel sounds for a word wall

Setup

Display the chart paper poem you created for "Singing Ducks" (see Using the Poem, above).

Directions

1 Reread the poem with children, pointing to the short vowel words (*ducks, nests*) or syllables (*yell* in *yellow, sill* in *silly*) as you go. Explain that the vowel sounds in these words are called short vowel sounds: Unlike long vowel sounds, they do *not* sound like the letter name of the vowel.

2 Read through the poem several times, focusing on a different short vowel sound each time. As you locate words and syllables for each short vowel (there are many non-Dolch short vowel words in the poem as well), have children repeat them after you.

3 Invite children to create a Short Vowel Word Wall. Provide children with index cards and help them find words in the poem that contain *only* short vowel sounds. Words can contain one short vowel syllable (*duck*) or more than one (*rabbit*).

4 Have children write the short vowel words on the index cards and post them on a bulletin board, grouping by sound. You can add to the word wall as children come upon new short vowel words in their reading.

Short Vowel Show

Objective

❧ to perform a readers' theater version of the poem

Setup

❧ Duplicate the poem "Singing Ducks" (page 99) and distribute one copy to each child, along with highlighter pens. Divide the class into groups of four children each. (If you have children left over, some can double up for a few speaking parts.)

Directions

1 Once children are grouped, assign each child a role for the performance: Narrator, Duck 1, Duck 2, and Duck 3.

2 Explain that Narrator 1 will read the title and the first stanza, and each Duck will read the speaking lines (indicated in quotation marks) for his or her stanza; and the whole group will read the last stanza together.

3 Help children in each group locate their lines and mark them with a highlighter pen. Give children plenty of time to practice their lines. Circulate among groups to check on children's fluency and provide assistance as needed.

4 When the groups are ready, have each put on a show! Rotate to let each group of children perform their version of the piece. Children not "onstage" can act as audience members, or you might even invite another class to see the performances.

Sight Word Focus

Words With Short Vowel Sounds

MATERIALS

○ copies of page 99 (one per child)

○ highlighter pens

Fox, Fox, on the Run

Sight Word Focus

Words With Short
Vowel Sounds

MATERIALS

- copies of page 103 (one per child)
- pencils
- index cards
- markers

Answers

Short A Words: *pat, cat, that, lap, has, and, chat, nap*

Short E Words: *head, when*

Short I Words: *hill, it's, still, sits, think, wink, its, it, think, pumpkin*

Short O Words: *fox, on*

Short U words: *run, cut, rub, upon, up, pumpkin*

Objective

❧ to identify in a song words with short vowel sound words

❧ to sort words by short vowel sounds

Setup

❧ Duplicate copies of the "Fox, Fox, on the Run" song sheet (page 103) and distribute one to each child.

❧ Create five columns on the chalkboard. Give each column one of the following headings: Short A, Short E, Short I, Short O, Short U.

Directions

1 Begin by singing the song "Row, Row, Row Your Boat" with children. Once they are familiar with the tune, direct children to their song sheets and practice singing "Fox, Fox, on the Run." Sing the song several times, until children are comfortable with the words.

2 Next, give each child a pencil and invite children to identify short vowel words in the lyrics by circling each one. Tell children that the words can be one syllable or more than one syllable, but they can contain *only* short vowel sounds. You might go through the first verse as a class to model the procedure.

3 When children are finished, draw their attention to the five vowel categories on the board. Have volunteers take turns writing the short vowel words they found under the appropriate heading. For instance, *fox* would go in the Short O column; *run* in the Short U column; and so on. (For complete answers, see left. Note that *pumpkin* can be placed in two different columns; short U and I.)

4 When your board is complete, provide children with index cards and markers. Let each child choose a few words to write on the cards and then add them to your Short Vowel Word Wall (see Activity 1, page 100).

Fox, Fox, on the Run

Sing to the tune of "Row, Row, Row Your Boat"

Fox, fox, on the run,
Softly down the hill.
It's a long, long way to home.
So you're running still!

Pat, pat, pat the cat
That sits upon your lap.
He purrs, meows, and has a chat,
And curls up for a nap.

Cut, cut, cut the pumpkin,
Its face looks real, we think.
We shake our heads and rub our eyes
When we see it wink!

Neighborhood Noise

This dog and **this** cat
Live in my house.
They like it here.

But **that** dog and **that** cat
Live with my friend Mike.
They like it over there.

These rabbits and **these** birds
Live in my yard.
They like it over here.

But **those** rabbits and **those** birds
Live in **that** yard.
They like it over there.

But **this** dog, and **that** dog,
This cat, and **that** cat,
These rabbits, and **those** rabbits,
These birds, and **those** birds,
ALL make lots of noise—perhaps you've heard!

Perfect Poems for Teaching Sight Words Scholastic Teaching Resources

Write the poem "Neighborhood Noise" on chart paper, using a different-colored marker to highlight the words *this*, *that*, *these*, and *those*. Read the poem aloud with children, emphasizing the highlighted words. For instructions on sharing poems, see pages 8–9.

Activity 1

This, That, These, and Those

Objectives

🌸 to recognize *this* and *these* as referring to items close by

🌸 to recognize *that* and *those* as referring to items farther away

🌸 to correctly use *this*, *that*, *these*, and *those* in sentences

Setup

Display the chart paper poem you created for "Neighborhood Noise" (see Using the Poem, above).

Directions

1 After reading the poem once through with children, discuss each stanza one at a time. In the first stanza, discuss the use of *this* in the phrase *this dog*. Ask: *How many dogs?* (one) *Where is the dog? Is it nearby or far away?* (nearby) Then ask similar questions about *this cat*.

2 Repeat the procedure for each stanza, focusing on each new highlighted word. Lead children to see that *this* and *that* refer to one (singular), and *these* and *those* refer to more than one (plural). Also point out that *this* and *these* refer to nearby things, while *that* and *those* refer to things farther away.

3 When children are familiar with the concepts, invite them to write their own four sentences, having them use one of the four target words in each. You can post children's work on a bulletin board for discussion.

Sight Word Focus

This, That, These, Those

MATERIALS

○ paper

○ pencils

○ copies of page 107
(one per child)

○ copies of page 108
(one per child)

○ crayons

○ pencils

Activity 2

Josh and Linda's Camping Fun

Objective

❋ to use picture and language clues to correctly complete sentences with *this, that, these,* or *those*

Setup

Duplicate pages 107 and 108 and distribute one of each to each child, along with pencils and crayons. Write *this, that, these,* and *those* on the board.

Directions

1 Invite children to look at the picture of Josh and Linda's campsite (page 107). Point out that it is pictured from above. They can color the river with crayons, if they wish. Ask: *What things can you see on Josh and Linda's side of the river? What can you see on the other side?*

2 Next, turn children's attention to the camping story (page 108). Read the introductory paragraph aloud. Explain that children can use both the picture and the other words in each sentence to help them decide which word fits best in the blank.

3 Try completing the first sentence as a class. Then let children complete the remaining sentences on their own. (For correct answers, see below.)

4 As an extension activity, older children might enjoy adding their own pictures to the campsite scene. Invite them to draw items (such as fishing poles and marshmallows) on both sides of the river. They can then write their own sentences about the items using *this, that, these,* and *those.*

Answers: 1. *this* 2. *that* 3. *this* 4. *that* 5. *those* 6. *these* 7. *those* 8. *these* 9. *this* 10. *that*

Josh and Linda's Campsite

Josh and Linda's Campsite

Josh and Linda set up their campsite before a rainstorm upset their plans. Now their campsite is divided in half by a river, and they cannot get across! Help Josh and Linda complete the sentences below. Fill in each blank with *this*, *that*, *these*, or *those*. Use the picture of the campsite to help you.

1. We can use _____ tent right here, on our side of the river.

2. We can't use _____ campsite over there, across the river.

3. We can eat _____ food on our picnic table.

4. But we can't reach the food in _____ tree across the river.

5. We can't use _____ two cooking pots across the river.

6. But we can cook our food in _____ three pots.

7. We can't use _____ three blankets across the river.

8. It's lucky we have _____ two blankets here to keep us warm tonight!

9. It's also lucky that we are on _____ side of the river, instead of the other side.

10. We're lucky because we are here, and _____ big snake is over there!

The End

Perfect Poems for Teaching Sight Words Scholastic Teaching Resources

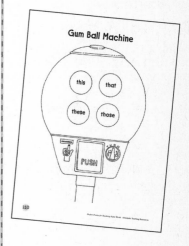

Gum Ball Machine

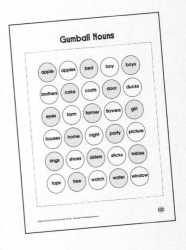

Gumball Nouns

The Gumball Game

Objective

❊ to use *this*, *that*, *these*, and *those* correctly with singular and plural nouns

Setup

Copy the Gumball Machine pattern (page 110) onto colored paper and glue it to the front of a paper bag. Then copy the Gumball Nouns reproducible (page 111) onto colored paper and cut apart the gumballs. Place the gumballs in the paper bag.

Directions

1 Invite each child to pick a random "gumball" noun from the bubble gum machine. Have children read their words aloud.

2 Next, invite children to look at the words printed on the outside of the gumball machine (*this*, *that*, *these*, and *those*). Ask: *Which two words can you use with the gumball you chose?* Lead children to see that if their noun is singular (*boy*) they can use it with *this* and *that* (*this boy*, *that boy*). If their noun is plural (*boys*) they can use it with *these* and *those* (*these boys*, *those boys*). Children hold their gumballs for the duration of the game.

3 Give each child two sentence strips. Have children write one sentence for each of the appropriate word combinations—for example: *This boy likes to play soccer. That boy likes to play baseball.*

4 Display children's completed sentences on a bulletin board and let volunteers take turns reading them aloud.

5 As an extension, cut circles of plain white paper and let children write their own singular and plural nouns. Add the new gumball nouns to the bubble gum machine and play again!

Sight Word Focus

This, That,
These, Those

MATERIALS

○ copies of pages 110–111

○ paper bag

○ sentence strips (two per child)

○ pencils

Gumball Machine

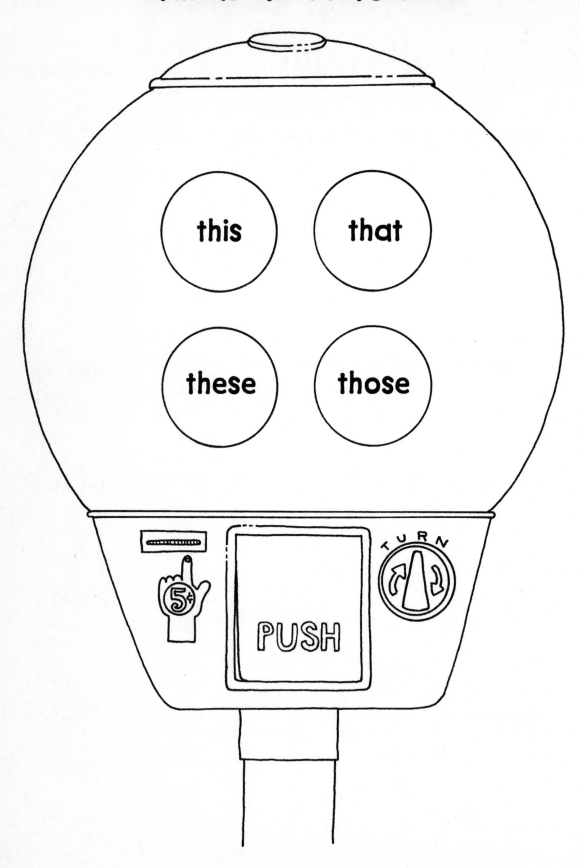

Perfect Poems for Teaching Sight Words Scholastic Teaching Resources

Gumball Nouns

apple　apples　bed　boy　boys

brothers　cake　coats　door　ducks

eyes　farm　farmer　flowers　girl

houses　home　night　party　picture

rings　shoes　sisters　sticks　tables

tops　tree　watch　water　window

References

Bridge, C., Winograd, P., and Haley, D. (1983) Using predictable materials versus preprimers to teach beginning sight words. *The Reading Teacher*, 36, 884-891.

McCormick, S. (1994). A nonreader becomes a reader: A case study of literacy acquisition by a severely disabled reader. *Reading Research Quarterly*, 29, 156-176.

McCormick, S. (1995). *Instructing children who have literacy problems*. Upper Saddle River, NJ: Prentice Hall.

Rasinski, T., and Padak, N. (2001). *From phonics to fluency: Effective teaching of decoding and reading fluency in the elementary school*. New York: Addison Wesley Longman.

Richek, M., Caldwell, J., Jennings, J., and Lerner, J. (2002). *Reading problems: Assessment and teaching strategies*. Boston: Allyn and Bacon.